Strategies
Challenging Behaviors
of Students with Brain Injuries

Written by
Stephen Bruce, M.Ed.
Lisa Selznick Gurdin, M.S.
Ron Savage, Ed.D.

BrainSTEPS

**Child and Adolescent Brain Injury
School Consulting Program**

Copyright © 2006 Lash & Associates Publishing/Training Inc.

All rights reserved. No part of this book may be reproduced, stored in a retrieval system, or transmitted in any form or by any means, electronic, mechanical, photocopying, recording, or otherwise, except for brief reviews, without the prior written permission of the publisher.

Published by Lash & Associates Publishing/Training Inc.
100 Boardwalk Drive, Suite 150, Youngsville, NC 27596-7761
Tel: (919) 556-0300   Fax: (919) 556-0900

This book is part of a series on brain injury among children, adolescents and adults. For a free catalog, contact Lash & Associates or visit our web site www.lapublishing.com

You may order this book directly from the publisher by calling (919) 556-0300 or visiting our website at www.lapublishing.com

Library of Congress Control Number: 2006925749

Table of Contents

About the Authors 3

Acknowledgments 5

Introduction 6

Overview 8

Chapter 1   Understanding the Brain and Brain Injury 9

Chapter 2   Common Behaviors following Brain Injury 17

Chapter 3   Overview of the Behavioral Approach 29

Chapter 4   Identifying and Defining Behavior 37

Chapter 5   Observing and Recording Behavior 41

Chapter 6   Types of Behavioral Assessment 55

Chapter 7   Practical Behavior Change Strategies:
             Manipulating Antecedents 83

Chapter 8   Practical Behavior Change Strategies:
             Providing Positive Consequences 87

Chapter 9   Case Studies 95

Conclusion 99

Glossary 101

References 105

Resources for Information 109

Appendix A: List of Blank Forms included on the separate companion CD . 113

Appendix B: Sample Case Using Completed Forms included on the separate
             companion CD 114

About the Authors

Stephen S. Bruce

Stephen Bruce, MEd, BCBA, CBIS is the Senior Director for Professional Development for the Neurosciences Institute at Bancroft NeuroHealth in Haddonfield, New Jersey. He earned a Master of Education degree in Applied Behavior Analysis from Temple University and is currently completing course work for a doctoral degree in special education from Temple University. Mr. Bruce coordinates staff training and development, teaches courses in applied behavior analysis at Temple University, and directs Bancroft NeuroHealth's professional conferences and workshops. He also chairs a behavior management committee and oversees school consultation services. Mr. Bruce has worked in the field of developmental disabilities and brain injury for the past 17 years and is a Board Certified Behavior Analyst as well as a Certified Brain Injury Specialist.

Lisa Selznick Gurdin

Lisa Selznick Gurdin, MS, BCBA, CBIS-CE is a part-time lecturer at Northeastern University and Chair of the American Academy for the Certification of Brain Injury Specialists (AACBIS) Board of Directors. Ms Gurdin is a Board Certified Behavior Analyst and an AACBIS Certified Brain Injury Trainer. She serves on the Board of Directors for the Brain Injury Association of America and supervises students for their associate behavior analyst certification.

She earned a Master of Science degree in Applied Behavior Analysis from Northeastern University. Ms Gurdin worked at the May Institute, Inc. in Massachusetts for eight years where she managed research and training grants, developed and coordinated a company-wide mentoring program, and taught courses in applied behavior analysis. She also has extensive experience designing and implementing home and school-based behavioral programming for children and adolescents with autism and brain injury.

Ronald C. Savage

Dr. Ronald Savage has worked with children, adolescents and young adults with neurological injuries and disabilities for over 25 years. Presently, Dr. Savage is Executive Vice President and Senior Author for Lash & Associates

Publishing/Training Inc. in North Carolina. Dr. Savage is the Executive Vice President of the North American Brain Injury Society. He is the former Executive Vice President of the Neurosciences Institute at Bancroft NeuroHealth in New Jersey, Senior Vice President of Behavioral Health and Rehabilitative Services at The May Institute in Massachusetts and Director of Clinical Services for Rehabilitation Services of New York.

In addition, Dr. Savage has taught at the elementary and secondary school level as a classroom teacher and as a special educator. He has also taught courses at several colleges and universities. Dr. Savage is the former Chairperson of the Pediatric Task Force for the National Brain Injury Foundation, the former Co-Chairperson of the International Pediatric Task Force for the International Brain Injury Association, and is a founding member of the American Academy for the Certification of Brain Injury Specialists.

Acknowledgments

We would like to thank a few individuals who helped us in the preparation of this manual. Kelly Sullivan spent many hours reading, editing, and proofreading parts of the manual. Karen Gould provided numerous suggestions. Thank you Kelly and Karen for all of your assistance and support. Our publishers, Marilyn Lash and Bob Cluett, were consistently patient and supportive during the creation of this manual. Our families deserve many, many thanks. They have given all of us their extraordinary love and encouragement. Finally, we could not have written this manual without the many students, families, and teachers with whom we have worked throughout the years. This manual is dedicated to you.

Introduction

In the United States each year, more than one million children sustain traumatic brain injuries (Brain Injury Association of America, 2000). Of those million...
- 7,000 children die
- 150,000 children are hospitalized, and
- 30,000 children experience lifelong disabilities.

❖ **Brain injury is the leading cause of disability in children between 1 and 14 years of age according to the National Center on Health Statistics (1999).**

Some students enter rehabilitation settings following a brain injury where they receive intensive treatment. Along with medical management, they may receive speech and language therapy, physical therapy, occupational therapy, vocational training, and special education. Rehabilitation goals typically focus on:
- improving mobility and self-care tasks,
- increasing cognitive and communication skills, and
- managing challenging behaviors.

Many children and youth with brain injuries are discharged directly home from hospitals and receive no rehabilitation services. Unfortunately, limited funding and insurance restrictions have resulted in shorter stays for those who do enter rehabilitation programs. Consequently, students often return to less restrictive and more challenging environments after their brain injury without the necessary skills to be successful at home, in school and in the community.

Students who sustain brain injuries often experience difficulties with attention, motivation, communication, learning, and thinking. As a result, every aspect of their lives, including academic performance, social interactions, and family relationships, may be significantly altered. Family members and teachers must respond to these new life changes every day. Changes in behavior and learning are often the most challenging deficits to manage following a brain injury.

This manual offers practical ways to successfully improve challenging behaviors, to promote effective learning strategies, and to teach functional skills at home, in school, and in the community. The recommendations that are presented are based on the principles of Applied Behavior Analysis (ABA). ABA is based on

over 50 years of research and offers a systematic approach to modifying behaviors. Behavior analysis provides the tools necessary to:
- determine why behavior occurs,
- identify positive strategies to reduce problem behaviors, and
- teach functional skills in a variety of settings and to maintain those skills over time.

ABA gives professionals in any discipline the tools to identify, define, and measure the effects of their treatments. By using these data-based methods, professionals may be both more efficient and more precise in determining the effects of their interventions.

Overview

This manual begins with an introduction to the relationship between brain function and behavior. To understand this relationship, Chapter 1 provides a description of how the brain works and how an injury disrupts the brain's functions. The area of the brain that is injured and the extent of the injury can greatly affect the way in which a student reacts to family and friends, performs academic tasks, and responds to daily life activities. Chapter 2 describes the challenging behaviors that commonly result from a brain injury and the impact of those behaviors on a student's daily functioning. Chapter 3 presents the guiding principles and methodologies of Applied Behavior Analysis. It is important that parents, educators, and professionals first understand the basics of behavior analysis in order to effectively use the behavioral approach to help students achieve treatment and educational goals.

The next three chapters are devoted to behavioral assessment. Behavioral assessment is essential both to determine why behaviors occur and to develop successful behavior support plans. Chapter 4 describes how to specifically identify and define behaviors. Chapters 5 and 6 describe the various types of behavioral assessment and emphasize the importance of observing and recording behaviors.

The second half of the manual provides parents and educators with practical behavioral techniques to reduce or eliminate unwanted behaviors that interfere with everyday activities. It also gives recommendations for how to incorporate these strategies into a student's Individualized Education Plan (IEP). Chapters 7 and 8 describe practical behavior change strategies that may be implemented in a home, school, residential, vocational, or clinical setting. Chapter 9 presents case studies that further illustrate how to incorporate the behavioral approach into a student's rehabilitation and/or educational program.

The appendices provide forms to help readers apply the techniques presented in this manual. These techniques are only examples of behavioral methods that are used to manage challenging behaviors and teach functional skills. There are many more strategies to explore. It is important to remember to look at behavior not as "something to punish," but as "something to change". Just as there are methods to improve mobility and speech, there are ways to improve students' behaviors so they may be successful in all areas of life.

Chapter 1
Understanding the Brain and Brain Injury

Introduction

The brain is the supreme organ that directs everything an individual does. It makes it possible for a person to think, communicate, act, move about, create and BEHAVE. Behavior is a "product" of the brain and how the brain responds to the environment. Just as thinking, speech and movement can be disrupted by a brain injury, so too can a person's behavior. The way a student responds to other people, reacts to overwhelming tasks, or feels about himself can be dramatically altered by a brain injury. The example below shows how a student's performance may vary depending on the structure and format of each particular class.

Juan sustained a severe brain injury to his frontal lobes. Three years after the injury, he has difficulty working independently in his art class and completing assignments. He functions well in math class and reports that he knows exactly what he needs to do every day.

During art class, Juan has been getting in trouble with peers, talking back to his teacher, and walking out of the classroom. Art class involves unstructured projects in which students can work at their own pace. Lately, Juan feels that he never knows what he is supposed to do in art class.

By contrast, his math teacher states that he is doing well. His math teacher gives Juan a checklist each day with assignments that he needs to complete and checks on him every 10-15 minutes.

The brain is comprised of specialized centers that are connected by a complex system of pathways. The parts of the brain work together as an integrated unit. When any one component of the unit is not working properly, the entire system may be disrupted.

The brain is similar to a car in some ways. Cars are made of numerous parts and systems that must be in good condition in order to reliably transport people from one location to another. If one of the many components is broken, the car will not be able to safely transport its passengers. For example, if the windshield wipers are broken, it is difficult to drive in the rain. If the brakes are worn out, the car will not stop effectively. These conditions can be dangerous for the passengers as well as for other drivers on the road.

The same is true when any part of the brain is damaged. The entire brain may be affected. As a result, the individual with the brain injury may experience difficulties in one or several areas. For example, when the frontal lobes are affected, the individual may not be able to independently initiate or complete tasks or regulate emotions. As a result, emotional and aggressive outbursts may occur. Similarly, damage to the cerebellum may result in poor coordination and balance. Individuals with this type of injury may lose their balance and may hurt themselves or others.

What Happens to the Brain When it is Injured?

When a brain is severely jolted by an external force, it often reverberates, or in other words, bounces around like "jello" in a plastic bag. This movement causes the brain to rub against the jagged, sharp, bony ridges of the skull. As a result, blood vessels and delicate nerve tissues of the brain are stretched and torn. Major bleeding and swelling then occurs. As one could expect, the brain is often significantly changed as a result of this trauma.

Brain Geography

Some basic understanding of neuroanatomy and brain functioning is helpful when considering how a student thinks, moves, and behaves. The brain works as a complex system of interconnected parts and pathways. To visualize the brain's geography, take a "road trip" of the human brain from the bottom to the top. The major parts of the brain are:

Brain stem	Located at the top of the spinal column, the brain stem relays information in and out of the brain. It regulates basic life functions (i.e., respiration, blood pressure, heartbeat) and also acts as the "point person" for all incoming and outgoing information.
Limbic system	Located in the area on top of the brain stem, in the middle section of the brain, the limbic system is involved with regulating and controlling emotions.

Cerebellum   Located in the lower back of the brain, the cerebellum coordinates, modulates, and stores all body movement. It is responsible for coordination and balance.

Cerebral cortex   The cerebral cortex, or cerebrum, is the largest part of the brain and performs the highest levels of thinking, planning, organizing, and learning. The cerebrum is divided into two hemispheres, which are then subdivided into four lobes: frontal, parietal, temporal and occipital.

A Closer Look at the Cerebral Cortex

By far the most complicated structural component of the brain is the cerebral cortex. This part of the brain is responsible for high levels of thinking, such as learning, remembering, planning, and organizing.

The cerebral cortex is divided into two hemispheres. Although the hemispheres work together, they also display many processing differences. The *left hemisphere* processes information in a logical and linear manner which helps a student better understand and use language (speaking, reading, writing, calculations). The *right hemisphere* responds to information in a more holistic and spatial sense (shapes, faces, music, art).

The cerebral cortex is further divided into four lobes: frontal, parietal, occipital, and temporal. The lobes each have specific responsibilities but also work together as a coordinated unit. Because there are two hemispheres, the lobes also have both a left side and a right side involvement. This means that the right and left lobes (i.e., left frontal lobe and a right frontal lobe) each have specialized functions.

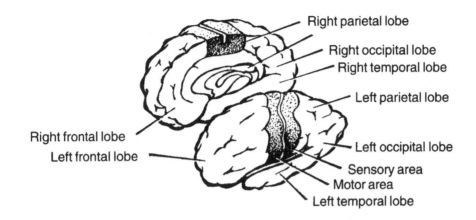

Frontal Lobes

The frontal lobes are particularly vulnerable to injury because they are located in the front part of the brain. Damage to the frontal lobes affect an individual's ability to organize information from the environment, prioritize, make decisions, initiate actions, control emotions, and interact with others. A student with a frontal lobe injury may not be able to "learn from mistakes" and so may repeat unwanted behaviors over and over again. It may seem as if a student's entire personality has changed.

Children and youth may not be able to control their behavior following a brain injury. This is because their frontal lobes are not responding at a level that is developmentally appropriate, not because they are intentionally misbehaving. Disciplining or punishing students with frontal lobe injuries usually does not help them understand or control their behavior. Rather, students should be taught strategies to compensate for their compromised frontal lobes. For example, students may learn to use daily planners and self-management tools to help them organize, plan, monitor, and complete daily tasks and activities.

Parietal Lobes

Spanning the brain like earphones are two adjacent bands of cortex: the ***motor cortex*** and ***somatic sensory cortex***. The motor cortex triggers movement whereas the somatic sensory cortex registers sensations. This motor sensory strip connecting the frontal and parietal lobes controls every voluntary movement from the simple pointing of a finger to coordinating the lips and tongue to make sounds. It is also the part of the brain that responds to touch, heat, cold, pain, and body awareness. Injury to the parietal lobe can cause a loss of these sensing abilities.

Occipital Lobes

The occipital lobes act as the primary visual center. Damage to the occipital lobes affects an individual's ability to correctly "see" and perceive the world. Consequently, a student with damaged occipital lobes may respond inappropriately to people and events.

Temporal Lobes

The temporal lobes rest on both sides of the brain and are the centers for hearing and language. New research suggests that the temporal lobes may also be the area of the brain in which memories are permanently stored. Students with brain injuries often have difficulty learning new information but maintain a good memory for information learned prior to the injury. Their memory system for understanding, storing, and/or retrieving new information is disrupted by an injury to this part of the brain. When students have attention, concentration, and memory problems, they typically have difficulty connecting new information with prior knowledge. Thus, functioning in every day life may be significantly affected.

Brain Development

Throughout the past decade, new technological advances such as magnetic resonance imaging (MRI) and special uses of electroencephalography (EEG) have helped researchers dispel earlier beliefs about the brain and learn new information about how a child's brain grows and matures. For example, the earlier belief that younger children with brain injuries experience more substantial recovery than older children after treatment is simply not true. Children and youth with brain injuries often have cognitive and behavioral challenges that last throughout their lives.

Furthermore, recent developmental studies have identified five peak maturation periods. These periods show varying developmental increments depending on the region of the brain. The five peak maturation milestones are described next.

Ages 1-6 years
During this period of overall rapid brain growth, all regions of the brain – those governing frontal executive, visuospatial, somatic, and visuoauditory functions – show signs of synchronous development until about the age of 6. Children are perfecting such skills as forming images, using words, and placing items in serial order. They also begin to develop problem-solving skills.

Ages 7-10 years
At this point, only the sensory and motor systems mature. This continues until about age 7 ½, when the frontal executive system begins accelerated development. Beginning at about age 6, the maturation of the sensory motor regions of the brain peak just as children begin to perform simple operational functions, such as logical mathematical reasoning.

Ages 11-13 years
This stage primarily involves the elaboration of the visuospatial functions, but also includes maturation of the visuoauditory regions. By the age of 10, visual and auditory regions of the brain mature and children are able to perform formal operations, such as mathematical calculations. They also find new meaning in familiar objects.

Ages 14-17 years
During these years, successive maturation of the visuoauditory, visuospatial, and somatic systems reach their maturational peak within one year intervals of each other. In their early years, young people enter the stage of dialectic ability. They are able to review formal operations, find flaws with them, and create new ones. Meanwhile, the visuoauditory, visuospatial, and somatic systems of the brain are developing.

Ages 18-21 years
The final stage begins around 17-18 years of age when the region governing the frontal executive functions matures on its own. Young people begin to question information they are given, reconsider it, and form new hypotheses that incorporate their ideas. This development occurs in conjunction with rapid maturation of the frontal executive region of the brain.

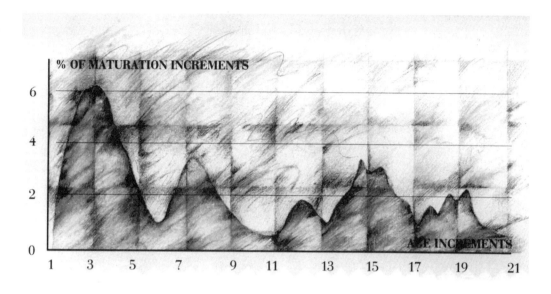

It is important to recognize that brain maturation occurs in immediate and abrupt changes during childhood. Thus, depending upon the child's age when injured and the region of the brain that is most affected, it may be possible to predict the kinds of cognitive and learning challenges that the child may experience immediately following the injury and years later.

For example, the three year old child who falls from a second story apartment and injures the frontal lobes may appear to fully recover within three to four months. However, as this child gets older and the brain continues to mature, the child may experience new cognitive or behavioral challenges when entering the secondary school years. This may occur as a result of damage to the frontal lobes. The student may not complete academic tasks, get into fights with other students, and may face serious disciplinary action. Unfortunately, educators may not even know about the earlier brain injury or may think that the injury has already healed. The student may then be labeled as a "behavior problem".

Conclusion

Knowledge about the long-term impact of an injury upon the developing brain will enable professionals to predict the resources that are necessary to help students with brain injuries successfully function in their everyday lives. By understanding brain-behavior relationships and the neurological changes that can occur following a brain injury, educators and therapists may better identify and understand a student's challenges.

The following sections of this manual describe practical behavioral strategies that may be used to help children and youth with brain injuries achieve their rehabilitation and educational goals so that they may lead productive and independent lives in their home, school, and community.

Chapter 2
Common Behaviors Following Brain Injury

Life after brain injury is never the same for either the youths who are injured or their families and friends. The student who is injured may not be able to engage in favorite activities (i.e., playing sports, musical instruments, games), have positive conversations with friends or family members, pay attention in class, or respond to the slightest change in routine. These challenges result from changes in how the brain functions. These changes may affect all areas of a student's life. Thinking, moving, communicating, being creative, hearing, seeing, and interacting with others may be severely impacted. Even the student's personality may change. Unfortunately, the brain can be changed forever when it is injured.

The most frequently observed unwanted behaviors associated with brain injury include inattention to task, aggression, perseveration, verbal outbursts, bolting, property destruction, noncompliance, and inappropriate sexual behavior. These behaviors can disrupt activities in the home, classroom, or community setting.

Challenging Behaviors

The behaviors described in this section are common and frequently result in difficulties for the student at home and in school. It is important for families and educators to understand that they are related to the brain injury.

Inattention to task

Students who have difficult attending to tasks may engage in unrelated tasks or behaviors. For example, they may fidget, talk out of turn, leave the room, instigate a fight with a peer, or stare out the window after a task has begun. As a result, the student may not complete tasks.

Failure to initiate tasks

Due to a frontal lobe injury, a student may have difficulty starting tasks. Instead, the student may engage in unrelated tasks prior to working on the original activity.

Aggression and destruction

Aggression and destruction can be dangerous behaviors. They may be directed towards teachers, peers, or family members. Students may even hurt themselves. Aggression/destruction may occur for several reasons. For example, a student may hit the teacher if frustrated by a difficult task or because of an inability to communicate effectively. Similarly, a student may throw an object or punch a wall in response to a teacher's demand or a peer's teasing.

Perseveration

Perseveration refers to repetitive speech about a particular topic. For example, a student may talk incessantly about cars, sports, or a TV show.

Inappropriate speech and verbal outbursts

Inappropriate speech may occur sporadically or in bursts. The student may use language that is not appropriate for the setting (i.e., saying "Hey man, what's up?" to a teacher). The student may also use obscenities.

Difficulty waiting

Students may no longer be able to wait appropriately. When required to wait (i.e., during transitions, before meals, while in-line at stores), these students may engage in any of the behaviors described above.

Age-inappropriate behavior

After a brain injury, a child's behavior may not mature at the expected pace beyond the age at the time of the injury. As the child gets older, interests may continue to be those of a younger child. On the other hand, a student may act older. Students may show an interest in sexual activities at a very early age.

Inappropriate sexual behavior

Inappropriate sexual behavior may involve making sexual advances to unknown peers, teachers, staff, or even family members. This behavior may involve making verbal sexual overtures or exhibiting nonverbal sexual behavior, such as touching and groping. Students with brain injuries often do not understand social rules, especially those regarding sexual behavior.

Bolting/elopement

Bolting, or elopement, means leaving a designated area without permission. Students with brain injuries tend to remove themselves from nonpreferred or aversive situations. Elopement can be a dangerous behavior if the student does not have safety awareness or good judgment in the community.

Noncompliance

Noncompliance is defined as refusing to follow instructions. For example, a student may be noncompliant by verbally refusing to do a task or by becoming aggressive. Noncompliance frequently occurs in response to nonpreferred or aversive tasks.

A **Challenging Behaviors Checklist** is included at the end of the chapter to help you identify your student's challenging behaviors. Use this checklist as part of the overall behavioral assessment provided in the appendix.

Causes of Behavior

There are many variables that cause or maintain these often debilitating behaviors. Initially, unwanted behaviors may be related to other physical, cognitive, and sensory deficits that are associated with brain injury. For example, verbal outbursts and physical aggression may be the direct or indirect result of frustration related to memory deficits, disorientation, slow processing, and/or poor communication skills. Challenging behaviors may also occur as a result of environmental factors, such as temperature, noise level, and lighting. For instance, a student who is sensitive to noise may bolt out of the room when several people in the room talk too loudly. Or, a student with an aversion to warm temperatures may show a tendency to be more aggressive during the summer.

❖ **Behavior usually is not the result of a single event, but a contribution of factors.**

Delayed Problems

Immediately following a brain injury, a student may appear to be unaffected by it. In fact, noticeable changes may not occur for several years. However, when everyday demands become more frequent or complex, behavior problems often emerge as the injured brain is challenged. Consider Sam's experience.

When he was 10 years old, Sam fell off his bicycle and had a moderately severe concussion. Although he lost consciousness for a few seconds, Sam did not seem to have any major consequences from the fall. Throughout his remaining elementary years, Sam did okay in school. His teachers reported that he was a bit hyperactive and needed help completing written assignments. However, his parents and teachers agreed that Sam's behaviors did not require special attention.

After Sam entered middle school, both his parents' and teachers' perspectives changed. Sam's grades worsened. He rarely started or completed assignments, was often disruptive during lectures, and frequently roamed around the school. Initially, his parents thought that Sam was having trouble transitioning to the new middle school environment. However, his behavior did not improve.

Sam's experience is familiar to many families of students whose brain injuries occurred during the elementary school years. Many of these students do not have difficulties until they are faced with learning new information, engaging in novel tasks, and adjusting to new situations. For some students, transitioning to middle school and then to high school is especially stressful. Challenging behaviors often emerge during these transitions. This may be due to the changing academic and social demands associated with the different settings. For example, in elementary school, students have only one primary teacher and they are seldom required to think analytically. Once students enter middle school, they change classes several times a day, interact with many teachers, and engage in abstract thinking and advanced problem-solving.

Most students experience difficult and tumultuous adolescent years. Students with brain injuries, who do not have appropriate cognitive and communication skills, may be completely overwhelmed by the academic and social demands associated with adolescence. They may "act out" verbally and physically. These behaviors may result in disciplinary action by school and community authorities. Students with brain injuries may also lose friends and have difficulty establishing new relationships.

Different Behaviors in Different Settings

As a general rule, students with or without brain injuries act differently in different settings and with different people. Remember when you were a child. When you were at home, you may have whined and tantrumed to avoid eating your broccoli, but when you were at a restaurant, you may have simply pushed the broccoli to the side. Similarly, you may have talked incessantly when you were with your family but became almost silent when you were with unfamiliar people.

It is not uncommon in team meetings for one person to report that a student does not follow instructions while another person claims that the student always follows instructions. It is also not uncommon for behaviors to simultaneously improve in one setting and become worse in another setting. Professionals address these issues by considering the environmental factors that exist in each setting. These factors may include the presence of particular teachers and peers, reward systems, task content, lighting, and room arrangement. Once the contributing variables are identified, the team can determine the best way to rearrange the variables so that the behaviors are less likely to occur.

Challenging Behavior Checklist

Student: _____ Date: _____

Evaluator: _____

    This checklist is designed to help you identify your student's challenging behaviors. The chart describes several behaviors and provides an example for each behavior. In the comments section of the chart, describe in more detail the specific behaviors that your student is displaying. Indicate if the behaviors occur simultaneously or in tandem with other behaviors. Circle the number that corresponds to the rating scale below. Behaviors that receive a 4 or 5 should definitely be addressed. List additional behaviors in the space provided at the end of the checklist.

Rating Scale

1 = never

2 = some of the time

3 = unsure

4 = most of the time

5 = all of the time

Challenging Behavior Checklist

Rating Scale

1 = never 2 = some of the time 3 = unsure 4 = most of the time 5 = all of the time

Behavior	Description	Comments	Rating
Inattention to task	Students who have difficulty attending to tasks may engage in unrelated tasks or behaviors. *Example:* A student may fidget, talk out of turn, leave the room, instigate a fight with a peer, or stare out the window after a task has begun.	_____ _____ _____ _____ _____ _____ _____ _____	1 2 3 4 5
Failure to initiate tasks	Due to a frontal lobe injury, a student may have difficulty starting tasks. *Example:* The student may engage in unrelated tasks prior to working on the original activity.	_____ _____ _____ _____ _____ _____ _____	1 2 3 4 5

Aggression	Aggression involves making physical contact with another person. It may include hitting, kicking, and punching and may be directed towards teachers, peers, or family members. Students may even hurt themselves. *Example:* A student may hit the teacher if frustrated by a difficult task or because of an inability to communicate effectively.	_____ _____ _____ _____ _____ _____ _____ _____	1 2 3 4 5	
Destruction	Destruction includes throwing objects and damaging furniture, walls, etc. *Example:* A student may throw an object or punch a wall in response to a teacher's demand or a peer's teasing.	_____ _____ _____ _____ _____ _____ _____ _____	1 2 3 4 5	
Perseveration	Perseveration refers to repetitive speech about a particular topic. *Example*: A student may talk incessantly about cars, sports, or the next visit home.	_____ _____ _____ _____ _____ _____ _____	1 2 3 4 5	

Inappropriate speech and verbal outbursts	Inappropriate speech may occur sporadically or in bursts. *Example:* The student may use language that is not appropriate for the setting (i.e., saying "Hey man, what's up?" to a teacher) or may use obscenities.	_____	1	2	3	4	5
Difficulty Waiting	The student may not able to wait appropriately. When required to wait (i.e., during transitions, before meals, while in-line at stores), the student may engage in any of the behaviors described above. *Example:* The student may leave the area, hit or kick the teacher, or start a fight with a fellow student.	_____	1	2	3	4	5
Age-inappropriate behavior	As the child gets older, his or her interests may continue to be those of a younger child. On the other hand, a student may act older. *Example:* Students may show an interest in sexual activities at a very early age (see inappropriate sexual behavior below).	_____	1	2	3	4	5

Inappropriate sexual behavior	Inappropriate sexual behavior may involve making sexual advances to unknown peers, teachers, staff, or even family members. *Example:* This behavior may include verbal sexual overtures or nonverbal sexual behavior, such as touching and groping.	_____ _____ _____ _____ _____ _____ _____ _____	1	2	3	4	5
Bolting/elopement	Bolting, or elopement, means leaving a designated area without permission. *Example:* A student leaves the school after being reprimanded by the teacher for verbal outbursts in class.	_____ _____ _____ _____ _____ _____ _____ _____	1	2	3	4	5
Noncompliance	Noncompliance is defined as refusing to follow instructions. *Example:* For example, a student may be noncompliant by verbally refusing to do a task or by becoming aggressive.	_____ _____ _____ _____ _____ _____ _____ _____	1	2	3	4	5

Challenging Behavior Checklist

Rating Scale 1 = never 2 = some of the time 3 = unsure 4 = most of the time 5 = all of the time

Additional challenging behaviors are:

Behavior	Description	Comments	Rating				
1.			1	2	3	4	5
2.			1	2	3	4	5
3.			1	2	3	4	5
4.			1	2	3	4	5
5.			1	2	3	4	5

General Comments:

Challenging Behavior Checklist

List the behaviors that were rated as a 4 or 5.

1. _____   Comments:

2. _____   Comments:

3. _____   Comments:

4. _____   Comments:

5. _____   Comments:

6. _____   Comments:

7. _____   Comments:

8. _____   Comments:

Chapter 3
Overview of the Behavioral Approach

Applied Behavior Analysis (ABA) has been successfully used to improve classroom learning, promote participation in community activities, facilitate positive social interactions, and increase independent completion of everyday tasks. For over six decades, researchers have systematically examined the environmental variables that affect behavior. They have conducted research in both the laboratory and clinical settings. This research has led to the development of the principles of behavior. Today, these principles are applied to change numerous behaviors in many settings, including classrooms, therapy sessions, hospitals, homes, and job sites. ABA has helped individuals with many diagnoses eliminate bad habits, take medication regularly, manage stress, and maintain an exercise regimen.

❖ **Applied Behavior Analysis (ABA) is concerned with understanding and changing behavior to significantly improve the quality of an individual's life.**

One of the most significant aspects of Applied Behavior Analysis is its systematic approach to treatment. The approach involves clearly and precisely defined goals, objectives, and treatment plans. Specific objectives are broken down into responses that can be described in detail, observed on an ongoing basis, and evaluated to determine progress. This avoids subjective statements about a treatment's effectiveness and a student's performance.

The behavioral approach offers professionals in any discipline a systematic approach to treatment. Allied health professionals, educators, and parents can incorporate this methodology when designing treatments, assessing skill development, and documenting improvement.

Behavioral Assessment

Behavioral assessment is one of the hallmarks of ABA. The purpose of a behavioral assessment is to systematically determine why behavior occurs.

❖ **Behavioral assessment involves objectively observing behavior in the natural setting. This is done to identify events that usually precede and follow the behavior.**

Environmental events, or variables, that lead to or maintain challenging behaviors include the following:
- Difficult assignments or tasks
- Peer or sibling behavior
- Noise
- Disruptions (i.e., someone walking in the door)
- Social attention
- Nonpreferred or aversive tasks or activities.

Once the significant variable(s) are identified, they are then changed or manipulated so that the behavior is less likely to occur in the future. For example, a student is observed throwing his pencils, verbally berating the teacher, and bolting out of the classroom every time a difficult math assignment is presented. Subsequently, the task is removed. The target behaviors (destruction, verbal outburst, bolting) appear to be caused by the presentation and termination of a challenging academic task. Further assessment looks at the components of the task as well as how it is presented. This information is considered to design the treatment procedure.

There are different types of behavioral assessment. These include staff and parent surveys, observations, descriptive analyses, and experimental manipulation. Chapter 7 is devoted to behavioral assessment. This chapter discusses the significance of behavioral assessment, describes different assessment methods, and addresses the role of behavioral assessment in the development of educational plans.

❖ **Without an assessment, treatment procedures may be ineffective. As a result, staff and family members may become frustrated, the target behavior may worsen, and additional behavioral challenges may emerge.**

Ongoing Data Collection

A fundamental component of ABA is objective and repeated direct measurement of behavior before, during, and after the implementation of a treatment procedure. Ongoing measurement allows the treatment team to objectively determine whether or not an intervention is successful and to avoid continuing an ineffective procedure or prematurely terminating a procedure that is working.

Objective	The behavior is defined in unambiguous terms so that all observers collect data on the same behavior.
Ongoing	Behavior is observed and compared throughout all conditions so that progress can be determined.
Repeated	An observer or observers record occurrences of the behavior during repeated observation periods.

Treatment Evaluation

In order to determine that a behavior has significantly improved, there must be a way to compare the new and improved behavior to the old behavior. This comparison involves observing and recording occurrences of behavior *before, during, and after* an intervention is implemented. Data that are collected before an intervention is implemented are called *baseline data*. Baseline data are then compared to data collected while the intervention is in place and after the intervention has ended.

❖ **Objective, ongoing, and repeated observation and measurement of behavior is necessary for behavior change to be documented.**

Graphing the Data

Once data are collected, they are visually displayed to objectively "see" the direction in which the behavior changed or if it did not change at all. Trends are data patterns that indicate whether or not the behavior is improving, remaining the same, or getting worse. Observation and measurement must continue until a trend is identified.

Trends are described as *increasing, decreasing, or staying the same*. The desired trend depends on the type of target behavior. If the behavior of concern is a problem behavior, the desired trend during the intervention phase is a decreasing trend. If the behavior is a newly developing appropriate behavior, the data should show an increasing trend during the treatment phase. In both cases, the trend shows that the behavior is improving.

Data are graphed during every phase of the behavior change process. This is done to evaluate the effectiveness of the treatment procedure. Data analysis addresses the following questions:

- Did the behavior change? If so, did it change in the desired direction?
- If the behavior changed, did it change immediately following the implementation of the intervention? In other words, was the intervention responsible for the change in the behavior or was it some other environmental variable?
- Did the behavior change in multiple settings?
- Was the behavior change maintained over time?

The results of the data analysis guide the team's decision-making regarding the effectiveness of the intervention and the degree to which the behavior improved. Graphs enable the team to inspect the data, identify the trend, decide whether or not to implement a behavior change procedure, and determine the extent to which the behavior improves as a result of the treatment procedure.

Changing the Environment to Change Behavior

Behavior analysis is based on the idea that behavior is primarily, but not exclusively, the result of changes in the environment. Therefore, behavior can be changed by modifying events that precede or follow the behavior. Environmental modifications may include adjusting activities, task requirements, and/or people's reactions to the target behaviors. Chapters 7 and 8 present several interventions that have successfully improved different behaviors in different settings.

Fair Pair Rule

The Fair Pair Rule states that for every problem behavior that is significantly decreased, at least one appropriate alternative behavior should be strengthened. This rule is important because it emphasizes that treatment plans should account for improvements in the student's overall behavior. Plans should not focus only on behavior reduction.

For example, behaviors that function as communication must be replaced by appropriate behaviors that communicate the same idea. If a student tantrums to express a need for a break, the student may be taught to present a break card instead.

Generalization and Maintenance

The ultimate goal of ABA is to change behaviors to a significant degree and to observe that change across settings, people, and time.

❖ **Generalization refers to improvements in behavior or newly trained skills that occur in untrained settings.**

For instance, the goal of an intervention designed to eliminate tantrums would only be considered successful if the frequency and intensity of the tantrums decreased in all settings in which they occur. In another example, the frequency of a child's social interactions increases with peers in the classroom setting even though social skills training was conducted in a separate training room.

❖ **Behavior analysts seek to identify behavior change procedures that are effective with a variety of individuals in a variety of settings.**

Maintenance refers to behavior change that continues when the treatment has ended. Behaviors that change only for a short time are not considered meaningful. For example, teaching a student to zip a coat is not significant if the student can not zip a coat six months later or if the student can not zip more than one coat.

❖ **Behavioral programs that are designed to reduce or increase behaviors should include a plan for ensuring that the behavior changes are observed across settings, occur with new people, and continue over time.**

Case Example: Sally

This case illustrates a systematic approach for changing behaviors. In this example, the team objectively documents Sally's improvement in science class because the target behavior (getting out of seat or talking out of turn) is operationally defined and measured before and during the intervention. By doing so, the team is less likely to continue an ineffective procedure or prematurely terminate an effective procedure.

Sally had a traumatic brain injury when she was 8 years old. The injury primarily affected her frontal lobes. She attended public school with an aide who helped her throughout the day. Due to the injury, Sally had difficulty attending in class, especially science class. Her science teacher reported that during his lectures, she frequently either talked to other students or started reading a book. He was very concerned because her behavior was disturbing the other students. In addition, Sally's science grade was significantly lower than her other grades.

Sally's team of teachers, her aide, her parents, and the behavioral consultant discussed the situation at the upcoming team meeting. They worked together to objectively define the target behavior, which they labeled off-task behavior. Sally's <u>off-task behavior</u> was defined as "talking when someone else is talking or being out of the chair." Then the aide quietly observed Sally during every 40-minute science lecture. She recorded the events that happened before and after the behavior occurred. In addition, the number of times, or frequency, of <u>off-task</u> behavior were recorded and graphed.

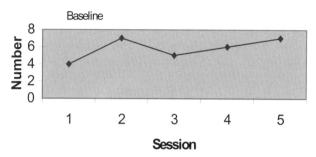

Off-Task Behavior

After reviewing the data, the team discussed possible explanations for the behavior. They discussed what happened before and after the behavior occurred, the seating arrangement, and the content of the lecture.

They discovered that the lecture material was probably difficult for Sally to follow and comprehend. They also determined that the teacher stopped the lecture to tell Sally either to sit down or to be quiet.

By evaluating the data, the team was able to identify two contributing variables: (1) the challenging content of the lectures and (2) the termination of the task following the occurrence of the behavior.

The team designed an intervention that addressed both variables: (1) the teacher would give Sally written lecture notes, and (2) the teacher would not stop the lecture when Sally talked out of turn or got out of her seat but would praise other students for paying attention. If Sally became too disruptive, the teacher or aide would nonverbally guide her back to her seat.

The aide continued recording the frequency of off-task behavior while the intervention was implemented. Again, these data were graphed (see the graph below) to show that Sally's off-task behavior decreased when the intervention was implemented. The team was also able to document that Sally's behavior improved and that it improved as a result of the intervention.

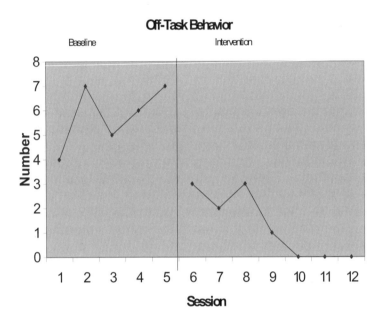

Chapter 4
Identifying and Defining Behavior

Students may have several behaviors following a brain injury, that interfere with everyday activities. It is critical that the entire educational team be involved to identify and prioritize target behaviors. Each member offers different expertise and a different perspective on the student and on brain injury.

At times, members of the treatment team may have different ideas about which behaviors should be identified for change. Or, they may agree on a list of problem behaviors but not concur on which behaviors to change first. The following checklist can be used to discuss and prioritize behaviors of concern.

Identifying Specific Target Behaviors
- Is the behavior harmful to the student or to others?
- How frequently is the behavior exhibited?
- Does the behavior interfere with everyday activities, such as activities of daily living, academic tasks, or transitions?
- Does the behavior limit positive interactions with peers, staff, and/or family members?
- Is the behavior age-appropriate?
- Does the behavior have a long history of occurrence?
- Is the behavior a problem for staff, therapists, teachers, or family members?
- Does the behavior lead to a chain of other challenging behaviors?
- Does the behavior limit community outings?
- Does the behavior interfere with the achievement of rehabilitation and/or educational goals?

It is just as important to teach adaptive skills as to reduce or eliminate unwanted behaviors. When deciding which positive behaviors and adaptive skills should be taught, consider the following questions:

- Will the skill/behavior lead to more positive interactions with peers, staff, and/or family?
- Is the skill/behavior just as easy to perform as the unwanted behavior?
- Will the skill/behavior lead to more social opportunities?

- Will the skill/behavior lead to more experiences in the community?
- Is the skill/behavior a prerequisite for other skills/behaviors?
- Is the skill/behavior age-appropriate?
- Will the skill/behavior assist in achieving rehabilitation goals?
- Will the skill/behavior start a positive chain of behaviors?

After the target behaviors have been identified and prioritized, the next step is to define the behaviors.

Clearly Defining Target Behaviors

In ABA, both the target behaviors and the intervention procedures are precisely defined. Definitions that are completely and thoroughly defined are referred to as operational definitions.

❖ **An operational definition is an observable, measurable, objective and unambiguous description of the target behavior.**

An operational definition describes the topography of the behavior; that is, what the behavior looks like. It includes examples of what the behavior is and what the behavior is not.

❖ **Topography is the form of the behavior or what the behavior looks like.**

Operational definitions are important because they allow the rehabilitation team to:

(1) accurately identify and measure target behaviors and
(2) apply the intervention procedures correctly and consistently.

Subjective definitions, on the other hand, do not clearly state the critical features of the behavior. As a result, observers may not identify the correct target behavior. Two observers may collect data on two different behaviors. Thus, their data cannot be compared. The data that are collected become meaningless.

The next table shows operational definitions as well as subjective definitions. Both types of definitions are included to illustrate their differences. Keep in mind that the label of the behavior is not as important as the definition itself.

Behavior	Subjective Definition	Operational Definition
Self-injurious behavior	Any time the student hurts himself.	Any time the student bangs his head against another surface (i.e., wall, chair, sofa). Does not include when the student touches or hits his head with a part of his body.
Off-task behavior	Any time the student is not doing what she is supposed to be doing.	Any time the student looks away from her paper, places the pencil on the desk, gets up from her chair, or initiates an interaction with a peer. Does not include when the student responds to a direct question or comment from the teacher, responds to a peer's comment or question, or picks up the pencil if it drops.
Cooperative behaviors	Any time the student shares with another student.	Any time the student offers a toy, crayon, or other play object to a peer, or gives the play object to a peer when asked. Does not include instances when the student initially refuses before giving the toy to the peer.

Once the target behaviors are operationally defined, the most effective method for measuring and evaluating the behavior is decided.

Chapter 5
Observing and Recording Behavior

It can be difficult for teachers and parents to be objective when discussing their student or child's problem behaviors because they are often the ones who are dealing with the behaviors on a daily basis.

Behavioral data collection involves observing the behavior and recording specific dimensions of the behavior. This systematic method enables the team to objectively measure the behavior, identify what is causing or maintaining the target behavior, decide how to most effectively change the behavior, evaluate the effectiveness of the intervention, and document the student's improvement.

Data collection helps the team:

- Identify variables that are associated with the target behavior
- Develop an effective intervention
- Document a student's progress
- Determine the success of an intervention
- Avoid implementing an ineffective procedure
- Avoid discontinuing a successful procedure.

Data collection should be done at scheduled times and should be collected in all settings in which the behavior occurs.

❖ **Observations should be conducted at the same time each day or each session so that the data are comparable across observation periods.**

Data Collection Methods

Data collection can seem like an overwhelming and impossible task. However, there are several efficient data collection methods that are practical and easy to use in a busy classroom or at home. These methods include frequency, duration, momentary time-sampling, percent occurrence, and permanent product. Each method is briefly described with sample data sheets to illustrate how data are recorded and graphs to show how data are displayed.

Frequency

Definition   The number of times a behavior occurs during a specific period of time. Recording the frequency that a behavior occurs is one of the most popular recording procedures for taking data.

Procedure   A mark is made on the data sheet when the behavior is observed.

<u>Sample Data Sheet</u> Frequency may be recorded during specific time periods or throughout the entire day or session.

Student: _____
Target Behavior: _____
Definition: _____
Observation Day(s)/Time(s): _____

Date	Observer	Frequency	Total Frequency

Example

Student: Jesse
Target behavior: Aggression
Operational definition: Any instance in which the student hits, kicks, grabs, or pulls the hair of another individual. The student must make contact with the individual.
Observation Day(s)/Time(s): Every day, 9-10:00 a.m.

Date	Observer	Frequency	Total Frequency
9/5	SK	11 111	5
9/6	SK	11 11111	7
9/7	LP	111 1 1	5
9/8	LP	1 1 1 1	4
			24

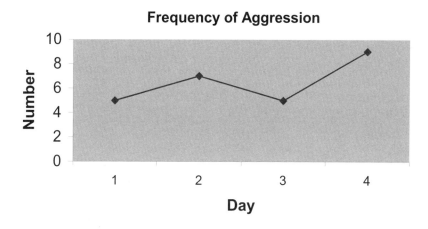

Duration

Definition The time between when the behavior starts and when it ends.

Procedure Duration measures can be collected as a total duration or duration per episode. Duration per episode measures provide information on how many times a behavior occurs in a particular time period (frequency) as well as how long the behavior continues (duration).

Sample Data Sheet

| Date: |
| Staff: |
| Target behavior: |
| Operational definition: |

Episode	Time in seconds
1	
2	
3	
4	
Total Duration:	

Example

Date: 2/4/03 Staff: DP Target behavior: Independent play Operational definition: An episode begins when the student begins manipulating a play object and ends after 5 seconds of no manipulation of that play object.	
Episode	Time in seconds
1	25
2	55
3	120
4	56
	Total Duration: 256 seconds or 4.27 minutes

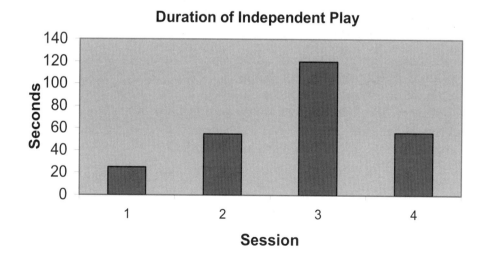

Momentary Time Sampling

This method is recommended for classroom teachers who must simultaneously attend to several tasks. Teachers often use this method to collect data on classroom behaviors, such as cooperative play, in-seat behavior, and on-task behavior. MTS is also suggested when collecting data on several behaviors or several individuals.

Definition Momentary Time Sampling (MTS) measures the occurrence of behavior at the end of a time interval (i.e., 5 minutes, 30 minutes). That is, the behavior is only observed and recorded after an interval ends. Data are reported as the percentage of intervals in which the behavior occurred.

Procedure The observer only records the occurrence or nonoccurrence of the behavior at the end of specific intervals. During the interval, the observer may attend to many different tasks during that interval (i.e., help students, prepare materials, lecture).

For example, a teacher who is interested in improving the on-task behavior of five students may use a momentary time sampling procedure. This procedure allows the teacher to collect data on all five students at the end of the intervals while preparing lecture materials during the intervals.

The 40-minute class period is divided into 7-minute intervals. On-task behavior is recorded only at the end of the interval. An auditory cue (i.e., prerecorded beeps) is used to signal the end of the interval. At the sound of the cue, or beep, the teacher looks up from her desk and records which students are on-task and which students are off-task. The teacher resets the interval and returns to her work. Seven minutes later, she repeats the procedure.

Student: Tina, Jim, Lori, Kathy, David
Staff: KO
Date: 5/8/03
Recording Code: + on-task; -- off-task
Recording Period: 10-10:40 pm
Interval Size: 7 minutes

Student	Interval				
	1	2	3	4	5
Tina	+	--	--	+	+
Jim	--	+	--	+	--
Lori	+	--	--	+	+
Kathy	--	--	--	+	--
David	+	+	+	--	--

Percent of On-Task Behavior (calculation: (#on-task/total intervals) X 100)
    Tina: 60%
    Jim: 40%
    Lori: 60%
    Kathy: 20%
    David: 60%

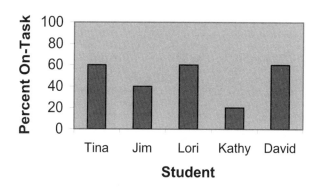

Sample Data Sheet

Observations of several behaviors.

Student:_____
Staff: _____
Date: _____
Recording Code:

Recording Period:
Interval Size:

Behavior	Interval				

Example

Student: Joey
Staff: KD
Date: 7/8/03
Recording Code: + behavior occurred; X behavior did not occur
Recording Period: 2:00 – 2:25 pm
Interval Size: 5 minutes

Behavior	Interval				
	1	2	3	4	5
On-task	+	+	+	X	+
Off-task	X	X	+	+	X
Cooperative behavior	X	+	X	X	+
Disruptive behavior	X	X	X	+	X

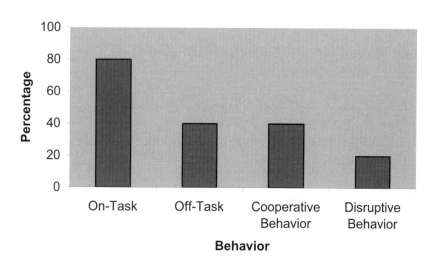

Percent Occurrence

Definition Percent occurrence is used when the opportunities to respond or to exhibit a behavior vary. Greetings, completing assignments, and answering questions are examples of behaviors that are exhibited in response to environmental events, such as an instruction. For example, a student answers a question when asked and responds to a greeting only when someone says, "Hello."

Procedure Percent occurrence is calculated by dividing the student's correct or incorrect responses by the total opportunities and multiplying by 100. The data are then re-ported as percent occurrences. For example, a student answers 10 out of 20 questions correctly one day and 8 out of 10 questions correctly on another day. The data would be 50% correct responding on Day 1 and 80% correct responding on Day 2.

Sample Data Sheet

Student: Date: Response:			
Date	Number Correct	Total Opportunities	Percent Correct

Example

Student: Peter Response: Correct answers to math assignments.			
Date	Number Correct	Total Opportunities	Percent Correct
8/9/03	8	10	80%
8/10/03	15	18	83%
8/11/03	9	12	75%
8/12/03	8	14	57%
8/13/03	10	15	67%

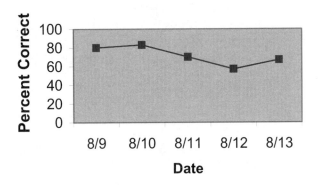

Percent Correct on Math Assignments: Peter

A Word about Data Sheets

Data sheets should be simple and easy to use. They should include the student's name, observer's name, date, setting, and target behavior(s). Operational definitions may be included or presented on a different form. In addition, the recording code should be included when measuring multiple target behaviors or observing multiple students. The recording code is the symbol system that is used to indicate the different responses that are being measured on the same data sheet. For example, on-task behavior may be indicated by a plus sign and off-task behavior may be indicated by a minus sign.

Choosing the Appropriate Data Collection Method

It is important to select the most appropriate method for data collection. When deciding which data collection method to use, consider the following questions:

- Is the behavior discrete? In other words, does the behavior have a definite beginning and end (i.e., obscenity, hand-raising, greeting, praise)?
- Is the behavior continuous (i.e., humming, rocking, hand flapping)?
- Does the behavior occur at a low, moderate or high rate?

The following worksheet is included to help you determine the most appropriate data collection method.

Choosing Method for Data Collection

Method	Type of behavior		Rate			Number of Students or Behaviors	
	Continuous	Discrete	Low	Moderate	High	1	>1
Frequency		X			X	X	
Duration	X			X		X	
Momentary Time-Sampling (MTS)	X	X		X	X	X	X

Examples

Target Behavior	Type of behavior		Rate			Number of Students or Behaviors		Method
	Continuous	Discrete	Low	Moderate	High	1	>1	
Aggression		X	X			X		Frequency
Noncompliance		X		X		X		Frequency
Cooperative play	X			X		X		Duration or MTS
On-task behavior		X		X			X	MTS
Verbal outburst		X			X	X		Frequency Duration

Sample Form

Target Behavior	Type of behavior		Rate			Number of Students or Behaviors		Method
	Continuous	Discrete	Low	Moderate	High	1	>1	

Making Data Collection Easy

Data collection does not have to be an arduous task. There are several efficient data collection tools that teachers and parents can use to make observing and recording data relatively easy. These devices are inexpensive and do not interfere with other tasks, such as attending to other students or making dinner.

Frequency Data

There are several different tools that are used to collect frequency data. Two of the most common methods use a wrist counter and counts tokens.

Wrist counter	The observer clicks the counter after each occurrence of the target behavior. Total frequency is indicated.
Token counting	The observer moves coins, beads, or tokens from one pocket to the other pocket or puts the items into a jar to keep track of each occurrence of the target behavior.

Duration Data

A stopwatch is highly recommended for accurate duration measures.

Chapter 6
Types of Behavioral Assessment

Behavioral assessment is an essential and necessary step in designing effective interventions for students with unwanted behaviors in the classroom, therapy, home, or community setting. All behavior serves a purpose. Behavior may occur to get someone's attention, to stop another person's behavior, express dissatisfaction, communicate a desire or need, or escape or avoid a particular activity or task. Behavior may also occur because it feels good or alleviates pain and discomfort.

Behavioral assessment is designed to determine the specific purpose or function of behavior by systematically observing and recording all environmental events and conditions that may cause or maintain the behavior. These environmental variables are clues as to what function the behavior serves for the student.

There are four main functions of behavior:

- To escape or avoid an unpleasant task or interaction
  Getting away from a situation or task that the student finds unpleasant is a function of behavior. Unwanted behavior, such as running out of the classroom or becoming disruptive when the teacher gives a student an instruction (i.e., to start working), results in a short break for the student.
- To gain attention from other people
  Interacting socially with other people is a function of behavior. A student may bang the desk or yell in order to get the teacher's attention.
- To gain access to a tangible item
  Obtaining an item or gaining access to an activity is a function of behavior. A student may kick the wall until the teacher comes to her table and gets the lunch box that is across the room.
- To satisfy a sensory or biological need

Obtaining sensory input or stimulation is a function of behavior. A student may hum extremely loudly or rock in a chair for sensory stimulation.

Behavior analysis aims to reduce behaviors that interfere with learning, restrict access to the community, limit social relationships, and cause personal harm or injury. The goal of ABA is to promote behaviors that improve an individual's quality of life.

Recall the Fair Pair Rule: An alternative behavior must be selected to replace the unacceptable behavior that is being decreased. The alternative behavior should serve the same purpose or function as the unacceptable behavior. Suppressing unwanted or inappropriate behavior without teaching a replacement behavior does not help the student fulfill the original function of the inappropriate behavior (i.e., to escape, get attention, express dislike). For example, if a student throws food, he should be taught an acceptable way to express that he does not want to eat the food that is presented. A procedure must also be developed to stop the student from throwing food.

Implementing a treatment intervention without conducting a functional behavioral assessment for unwanted behavior is analogous to a pediatrician or speech language pathologist prescribing a treatment without seeing or assessing the child. Treating behavior in the absence of a behavioral assessment is rarely effective, especially in the long term. In many cases, an intervention eliminates an unwanted behavior for a short time; however, that behavior soon resurfaces because the intervention was not based on a behavioral assessment. Students with brain injuries and other disabilities have the right to effective behavioral assessment and treatment of unwanted behavior and other discomforts that have a negative effect on their quality of education and life.

Determining the function of unwanted behavior answers two critical questions:
o Under what circumstances does the unwanted behavior occur?
o Why is the individual engaging in the behavior? (i.e., What purpose does the unwanted behavior serve for the student?)

Unwanted Behavior as a Form of Communication

Communication is critical to everything that we do – speaking, listening, reading, writing, and talking with others. In many cases, unwanted behavior is a form of communication. Consider a student who throws his work and hits the teacher when presented with a math problem that is too difficult or too long or when he prefers to do another subject before math. A thorough functional behavior assessment can pinpoint the conditions or variables under which the problem behavior occurs. In turn, this information provides clues to the need that the behavior satisfies for the student. It is important to understand that it is the "form" of the unwanted behavior that is the problem, not the purpose or need that engaging in the behavior serves.

The goal of a functional assessment is to teach the student a socially acceptable replacement behavior to satisfy the student's needs.

❖ **Communication in its broadest definition really is behavior, and behavior in its broadest definition, really is communication.**

Communication-based strategies should focus on developing functional behaviors that are appropriate to the setting in which they should occur. Feeney and Urbanczyk (1994) recommend the following stages of behavioral assessment to better understand a student's communication needs:

- Operational description of language skills
- Standardized language assessment
- Functional assessment of communication and language
- Analysis of interactive ability of teachers/therapists
- Analysis of executive functioning skills (i.e., planning, organizing, initiating) and problem solving skills.

For example, a student who runs out of the room and becomes aggressive toward another person may be communicating frustration or confusion. This student should be taught appropriate strategies to recruit teacher attention, to express frustration (i.e., putting head down on the desk), or to exit a social situation when peer pressure is too demanding.

DePompei and Blosser (2000) list additional strategies to help teachers, therapists, and families support the communication needs of students before these needs become behavior problems:

Tips on communication
- Give instructions slowly and clearly.
- Use simple vocabulary and short sentences when giving important information.
- Give clear written instructions.
- Talk about familiar subjects.
- Introduce new ideas slowly.

Tips to prevent confusion
- Know the signs of confusion and frustration and intervene as soon as the signs appear.
- Explain confusing situations.
- Reduce distractions.
- Use pictures, written cues, gestures, and facial expressions to communicate to the student.

Tips on educating others
- Teach friends and relatives how to communicate with the student.
- Encourage special projects that capitalize on the student's strengths.
- Advocate for the student when there are difficulties with communication.

Assessment Methods

Unwanted behaviors are related to the events before and after they occur. *Antecedents* are the events that precede the behavior. *Consequences* are the events that follow the behavior. Behavioral assessment provides the tools to identify the antecedents and consequences that maintain the behavior by examining the environmental context in which behavior occurs. Several techniques can be used to identify the function of behavior. These techniques can be grouped into three categories: (1) indirect, (2) direct, and (3) experimental methods.

Indirect Methods of Assessment

These techniques rely on indirect means of gathering information in order to form a hypothesis about the function of the unwanted behavior. The word hypothesis is used here because indirect methods can only suggest or hypothesize a function because they do not involve systematic observation and analysis. Without such an analysis, the purpose of a behavior can only be inferred, not determined.

Information from indirect methods is used to identify the conditions for a systematic or experimental functional analysis. For example, indirect assessment methods provide valuable information about when and where to conduct direct observations.

❖ **Indirect methods identify the antecedents, consequences, activities, social settings, or academic environments that appear to be sustaining the unwanted behavior.**

❖ **Indirect methods include structured interviews, rating scales, student records, and checklists.**

These methods are very useful for developing a hypothesis about why the unwanted behavior occurs. However, they usually do not produce enough conclusive evidence to design an intervention that addresses the function of the behavior.

Structured Interviews

Structured interviews are designed for parents, caregivers, and staff. Interviews ask specific questions regarding the targeted behavior. The answers to these questions help determine when and where to perform direct observations. Below are sample questions from the interview format found in the appendix:

- In what settings/situations is the behavior most/least likely to occur?
- When (what times) is the behavior most/least likely to occur?
- Which activities are most/least likely to produce the behavior?
- With whom is the behavior most/least likely to occur?
- What usually happens right before the behavior occurs?
- What usually happens following the behavior?
- How do others react to the student and/or to the behavior?
- Do others attend to the student while is the behavior being displayed?
- Does the behavior allow the student to escape or avoid a particular situation?
- What actions seem to improve or stop the behavior when it occurs?

Interviews also include questions related to medication and medication changes. This is important because medications that have side effects (i.e., lethargy, drowsiness, fatigue, or noncompliance) can change a student's behavior. This information should be collected during the interview phase so that medical explanations for behavior can be eliminated.

Questionnaires and Assessment Scales

Questionnaires and assessment scales are more refined and quantitative than interview questions because they require an individual to rate behaviors using various scales. Many scales require the individual to rate how often a behavior occurs (i.e., never, seldom, most of the time, always). Each question that is rated is scored to produce a number that corresponds to several possible functions that an unwanted behavior may serve (i.e., escape, attention, tangible, sensory). The following questionnaires are commonly used to assess behavior:

- Motivation Assessment Scale (MAS) (Duran & Crimmins, 1988; 1992)
- Functional Analysis Screening Tool (FAST) (Iwata, 1996)
- Aberrant Behavior Checklist (Aman & Singh, 1994)

Below are a few sample questions from the Motivation Assessment Scale (MAS):

- Escape
  Does the behavior occur following a request to perform a difficult task?

- Attention
  Does the behavior seem to occur in response to you talking to other persons in the room?

- Tangible
  Does the behavior stop occurring shortly after you give this person the toy, food, or activity that has been requested?

- Sensory reinforcement
  Does it appear to you that this person enjoys performing the behavior? (It feels, tastes, looks, smells, and/or sounds pleasing.)

Similar to the structured interview, these rating scales help form a hypothesis about the relationship of the unwanted behavior to environmental events. This relationship is then further clarified by conducting Direct and Experimental Assessments. These assessments are discussed later in the chapter.

Direct Methods of Assessment

Also called descriptive methods, direct assessment methods involve direct observation of unwanted behavior in the environment or setting in which it occurs. For example, if the behavior occurs while the student is in social studies class, observations should occur during social studies. Likewise, data should be collected at a student's job site if the target behavior is displayed there. It does not make sense for observations to occur in settings in which the behavior does not occur.

With direct methods, an observer records the frequency, and sometimes duration, of the behavior as it occurs. The observer also records the antecedents that precede the behavior and the consequences that follow the behavior. Collecting data on antecedents and consequences as they occur helps to identify the environmental conditions that maintain behavior. Remember that these conditions provide specific clues as to the function or purpose of the behavior.

Direct methods are more valid and reliable than indirect methods because they involve direct observation of target behaviors *as they happen.* Unlike interviews and surveys, these methods do not rely on memory and recall of past events. The results of indirect methods, however, provide valuable information about specific events that should be observed during direct assessment methods.

Another advantage of direct assessment is that the observers can be the individuals who already interact with the student in that environment. Staff, teachers, therapists, and parents can collect these data with minimal training.

There are primarily two ways to conduct direct assessments: 1) antecedent-behavior-consequence (ABC) analysis and 2) scatter plot assessment.

Antecedent – Behavior – Consequence (ABC) Analysis

This is a process whereby events immediately preceding the targeted unwanted behavior and events immediately following the behavior are observed and briefly described. Data are collected using a data sheet similar to the next example.

Student:_____   **Observer:**_____

Date	Time	Antecedent	Behavior	Consequence	Comments
5/6/03	11:35AM	Asked to get ready for lunch	Hit staff	Physical restraint	10 min restraint
5/6/03	11:55AM	Asked to get ready for lunch	Hit staff	Blocked and redirected to sit quietly	Sat quietly until 12:15 PM
5/7/03	11:40AM	Asked to put books away	Hit staff	Asked to wait until other students leave for lunch	Left for lunch at 12:10 PM
5/8/03	11:45AM	Asked to get ready for lunch	Hit staff	Physical restraint	10 min restraint

In this example, the target behavior (hitting staff) occurred for three days (5/6, 5/7, 5/8) when staff asked the student to either prepare for lunch or to clean up his area prior to leaving the classroom to go to the cafeteria. These data also show that the target behavior occurred between 11:35 and 11:55 AM and that after each occurrence of aggression, going to lunch was delayed either by sitting and waiting or by being placed in a physical restraint.

Evaluation of the data suggests that the behavior may serve different functions:
1. to avoid going to lunch
2. to express a desire for the current activity to continue
3. to walk to lunch with a teacher.

This information is then used to develop the conditions in an experimental analysis.

Scatter Plot Analysis

Unwanted behaviors often occur in predictable patterns according to the day of the week and/or the time of day. These behaviors may also occur around specific activities and in the presence of particular individuals.

For example, a student may become aggressive only when a specific teacher is present or during the class period directly before lunch. Alternatively, a student may perform all of the activities involved in physical therapy but does not participate in speech therapy tasks. Scatter Plot Analysis helps to identify patterns of unwanted behavior that correlate with time of day or environmental events (Touchette, MacDonald, & Langer, 1985).

This analysis helps to determine behavioral patterns related to any of the following variables:
- Time of day
- Day of the week
- Presence of staff, family members, peers
- Instructional activities
- School classes
- Therapies
- Settings: school, community, home

A scatter plot analysis is done through visual inspection of the data, which are displayed in a grid such as the one following. This grid shows an example of a completed scatter plot. The grid shows a pattern of behavior that occurs during the transition period prior to lunch. For example, there may be a particular staff member who is present then. The student may also be attempting to avoid the noisy, busy, and chaotic hallway during the transition time. Based on these data, an experimental analysis focuses more closely on the events that occur during the time period directly prior to lunch and during the transition to lunch.

Scatter Plot Analysis

Date / Day of wk	Sun	Mon	Tue	Wed	Thur	Fri	Sat	Sun	Mon	Tue	Wed	Thur	Fri	Sat	Comments
7:00 AM															
7:30 AM															
8:00 AM															Bus
8:30 AM															Bus
9:00 AM															Circle
9:30 AM					X										Math
10:00 AM					X										Vocational
10:30 AM			X												Vocational
11:00 AM			X												ADLs
11:30 AM		■	■	■	■	■			■	■	■	■	■		Transition
12:00 PM						■							■		Lunch
12:30 PM															Lunch
1:00 PM															ADLs
1:30 PM															Vocational
2:00 PM															Transition
2:30 PM															Bus
3:00 PM															Bus
3:30 PM															
4:00 PM															
4:30 PM															
5:00 PM															
5:30 PM															
6:00 PM															
6:30 PM															
7:00 PM															
7:30 PM															
8:00 PM															
8:30 PM															
9:00 PM															
9:30 PM															
10:00 PM															

Instructions

Fill in each interval with ■ if the target behavior occurred more than once in the thirty minute interval
Fill in each interval with X if the target behavior occurred once in the thirty minute interval
Leave the interval blank if the target behavior did not occur in the thirty minute interval

The main advantage of using a scatter plot analysis is that it produces a consistent behavioral pattern that can easily be discerned by looking at the grid. Often these patterns are not apparent when reviewing traditional student records, questionnaires, or other data sheets. By highlighting a pattern, further assessment of the behavior can then address the potential conditions (i.e., specific times, people, places) in which the unwanted behavior typically occurs.

Descriptive Analysis

A descriptive analysis is conducted after information from an indirect assessment is gathered. It is a final part of the direct assessment methods. In a descriptive analysis, the assessor directly observes and records data during the times indicated by the ABC and/or the scatter plot. This analysis elicits more detail regarding the antecedent events occurring in the environment.

For example, in the half hour before lunch, specific conditions can be noted:
- Number of adults and students in the room
- Specific verbal prompts used
- Other students' behavior
- Lighting
- Temperature
- Interactions with staff
- Frequency of reinforcement for appropriate behavior

From this information, intervention strategies begin to emerge. For example, if the student consistently reacts to the transition to lunch by hitting staff, it is possible that the student needs several reminders that, "We will be going to lunch in 10 minutes." This reminder is then repeated 5 minutes later. Another possible strategy for decreasing the aggressive behavior is to modify the teacher's instructions. The teacher can start the transition by showing the student what is on the menu for lunch. Thus, the student attends to something preferred rather than focusing on discontinuing the current activity.

Experimental Methods of Assessment

Indirect and direct methods are helpful to develop a hypothesis about the function of the behavior. These methods identify the variables that most likely contribute to the occurrence of the target behavior. However, information gathered in these assessments only suggest behavioral function. There is not a high degree of certainty that the hypothesized function is accurate. As a result, treatment that is developed from the results of these assessments may or may not accurately address the the behavior's purpose or function. Treatments that do not match the function of the unwanted behavior are not as likely to be successful.

For example, the indirect and direct assessments may suggest that a student is inattentive to tasks because the task is too difficult. However, further assessments reveal that the the actual function of the behavior is to gain the teacher's attention. In this case, an intervention that addresses the difficulty of the task (by interspersing easier tasks with harder tasks) may not decrease the unwanted behavior. Nevertheless, in many cases, the information obtained from these methods is all that is possible given time and available resources.

In an ideal situation, the hypotheses that are formulated from indirect and direct assessments are tested in an experimental analysis. The term "experimental" indicates that certain variables or events are manipulated in order to verify a functional relationship between the unwanted behavior and the events that exist before or after it occurs. Does the behavior consistently occur or not occur when events are present or absent? In other words, when the event or variable is present, the behavior occurs; when the variable is not present, the behavior does not occur. If this is true, then there is a functional relationship between the behavior and those variables.

For example, a student engages in verbal outbursts only when another student enters the classroom. When the student is not in the room, the verbal outbursts do not occur. These observations suggests that there is a functional relationship between the student's verbal outbursts and the presence or absence of the other student.

During an experimental analysis, which is also called a functional analysis, events are systematically arranged to determine if problem behavior occurs consistently in those situations. This analysis allows for a more definitive statement about the function of the unwanted behavior.

❖ **There are two types of experimental analysis: antecedent analysis and consequence analysis.**

Antecedent Analysis
Antecedent analysis is one method of testing the hypothesis generated by indirect and direct assessments. Often called a structural analysis, it involves systematically presenting specific antecedent variables that have been identified to be associated with the unwanted behavior. These antecedent variables are also

called triggers because they prompt unwanted behavior by students (Rolider & Axelrod, 2000).

❖ **Antecedent variables are events, people, demands, or interactions that reliably precede the occurrence of unwanted behavior and appear to trigger it.**

During this analysis, the consequences for the unwanted behavior, or the events that follow unwanted behavior, are held constant. For example, direct assessment information suggests that a student occasionally exhibits aggression (i.e., hits, kicks, grabs hair) towards his teacher immediately after a math assignment is presented to him. In an antecedent analysis, different types of work (i.e., easy, difficult, or no work) are presented to the student during short sessions. This is done to assess whether or not there is a change in the occurrence of throwing the tasks and hitting the teacher based on the type of assignment given.

This information is then used to develop a successful intervention. If an antecedent analysis shows that there are no occurrences or significantly low rates of the unwanted behavior in the easy work conditions and high rates of the behavior in the difficult work condition, the treatment procedure may involve modifying difficult work assignments while initially presenting only easy work. Then more difficult tasks are gradually faded in.

The information below shows the definitions, data collection, and graphic display of the analysis used in the above example.

Condition: Math problem antecedent analysis				
Student: Susan				
Target behavior: Aggression				
Operational definition: Any instance in which the student hits, kicks, grabs, or pulls the hair of another individual. The student must make contact with the individual.				
	Session 1	Session 2	Session 3	Session 4
No Work	0	1	0	0

67

| Current Work | 11111 | 1111111 | 1111 | 11111 |
| Easy Work | 1 | 0 | 1 | 0 |

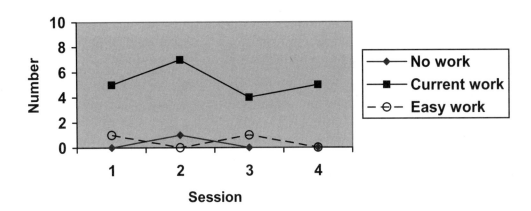

This graph suggests that the no work and easy work conditions result in low rates of aggression. This information is useful for developing an intervention such as the one described in the treatment effects analysis next.

Ideally, antecedent analysis would not be used exclusively because it does not assess the extent to which reinforcement may affect occurrences of the behavior. In the above example, the antecedent analysis does not specifically identify escape as a function of the behavior. This example only shows that easy math work or no work resulted in low rates of aggression. Thus, it can only be assumed that the student engaged in the unwanted behavior to avoid the current math assignment.

Consequence Analysis

This type of assessment involves presenting specific consequence variables that are associated with the unwanted behavior. These variables are systematically arranged in order to determine if the behavior occurs consistently in those situations. A consequence analysis is used to show a functional or controlling relationship between behavior and its consequences.

❖ **The reinforcing variable, or what the person is communicating, can be more accurately identified by evaluating the unwanted behavior across several different consequences.**

There are generally four functions or purposes that unwanted behavior serves for individuals (escape, attention, tangible, and sensory). Listed below are the conditions and session descriptions which are conducted in a consequence analysis. They correspond to the four functions of behavior.

Escape or Demand

This condition is conducted to determine if the function of the unwanted behavior is to escape, terminate, or avoid a task or situation that is unpleasant to the student. In this condition, the student is asked to complete a task, which the student has the skill to perform. If the targeted unwanted behavior occurs, the task is terminated or removed for 30 seconds before being presented again. This process is repeated for the duration of the session. A session usually lasts 5-10 minutes. Behavioral data are collected and graphed for each session (see example).

If the occurrence of unwanted behavior is significantly higher in this condition than in the other comparison sessions, then it may be that the function of the unwanted behavior is to escape demands or tasks. In this case, the behavior is maintained by negative reinforcement. In other words, the behavior is maintained because the task is terminated or delayed as a result of its occurrence.

Attention

The purpose of this condition is to determine if attention maintains the unwanted behavior. In this situation, the student is provided with attention from the teacher or a staff member for approximately 30 seconds following the occurrence of the target behavior. After 30 seconds, the teacher stops interacting with the student and engages in paperwork or some other task that does not involve interacting with the student. Attention can take the form of a mild verbal reprimand or other comment that is appropriate to the individual. This process is repeated for the duration of the session (5-10 minutes). Behavioral data are collected and graphed for each session.

If the occurrence of unwanted behavior is significantly higher in this condition than in the other comparison sessions, then it may be that the function of the unwanted behavior is to get the teacher's attention. This also indicates that the unwanted behavior is maintained by positive reinforcement in the form of teacher attention.

Access to tangible items

This condition is conducted to determine if access to a tangible item maintains the unwanted behavior. In this condition, the student is provided with access to the tangible item for approximately 30 seconds. After 30 seconds, the teacher removes the item or denies access to it. If the targeted unwanted behavior occurs, the item is again provided for 30 seconds. The item is withdrawn again after 30 seconds and the process is repeated for the duration of the session (5-10 minutes). Behavioral data are collected and graphed for each session.

If the occurrence of unwanted behavior is significantly higher in this condition than in the other comparison sessions, then it may be that the function of the unwanted behavior is to access preferred items. This would indicate that the behavior was maintained by positive reinforcement in the form of receiving a tangible item.

The item used in the session is selected based on information gathered from the interview process. Tangible items can include games, video or audio access, or food items. Food items should be only used if the student's family and/or pediatrician approve their consumption.

Sensory or automatic reinforcement

At times, the unwanted behavior is not related consistently to any one antecedent or consequence condition. In other words, the behavior occurs at various times and places in a seemingly random pattern. In this case, all of the above conditions do not show a functional relationship to the behavior. If rates of unwanted behavior occur consistently throughout all conditions, engaging in the unwanted behavior may simply feel good or it may alleviate some pain or discomfort.

To assess the sensory function of behavior, an alone condition is implemented. During this condition, the student is alone in a room for a short period of time. This is done to determine if the behavior occurs when the student is alone without demands and without access to attention or tangibles. It should be noted that this condition should not be used if repeated occurrence of the unwanted behavior is harmful to the student.

Control Session

In this session, the student has access to preferred toys and teacher attention on a frequent basis throughout the session. In addition, no demands are placed on the student. This condition is designed to trigger little to no occurrences of the target behavior. If unwanted behavior occurs consistently in this condition, the behavior may be serving a sensory or biological function.

The following sample analysis addresses the consequences of the scenario used in the antecedent analysis example above. Remember, the target behavior is aggression towards the teacher. The results of the indirect and direct assessments suggested escape from the current math work as a possible function for the aggressive behavior.

For this example, the steps of a consequence analysis are described below. The purpose of the demand session is to assess the extent to which negative reinforcement or escape from the task functions to maintain the target behavior. In other words, does the aggressive behavior occur because it allows the student to avoid math assignments?

<u>Consequence Analysis Steps</u>
1) Short sessions of 5 to 10 minutes are conducted.
2) Math work that is correlated with the unwanted behavior is presented.
3) The student is given a break from work for 30 seconds immediately following the display of aggression.
4) The task is represented after the 30 second break.
5) This cycle is repeated until the end of the session.
6) Several sessions are conducted until a pattern emerges.

Frequency data collection summary

Condition: Demand or negative reinforcement Student: Jamie Target behavior: Aggression Operational definition: Any instance in which the student hits, kicks, grabs, or pulls the hair of another individual. The student must make contact with the individual.			
Session 1	Session 2	Session 3	Session 4
ll 1 1 1	ll 111 11	ll 1 1	ll 1 1 1
Total: 5	Total: 7	Total: 4	Total: 5

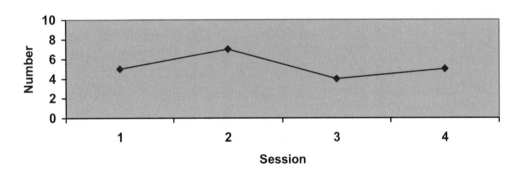

What does this graph tell us? High levels of unwanted behavior during the demand session suggest the hypothesis is correct that the student engages in the unwanted behavior to escape the task. However, it is necessary to compare data from the demand sessions to data collected during conditions (i.e., tangibles, attention, control). The graph below represents the results of this comparison:

Session Comparison

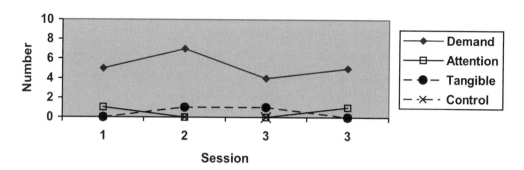

The above graph shows that aggression occurred significantly more often during the demand condition. These results support the hypothesis that the purpose of the behavior is to escape the task.

The results of the consequence analysis are considered to determine the intervention. In order for the behavior to successfully decrease, the treatment procedure must match the function of the behavior which, in this case, is escape. Treatment selection is a process that should follow a behavioral assessment whenever possible.

In the above example, one treatment option is Differential Reinforcement of Alternative Behavior (DRA) plus Extinction. This intervention procedure involves not allowing the student to escape or avoid the task (extinction) while reinforcing him for exhibiting a functional communication response, such as appropriately requesting a break. The specific DRA Plus Extinction procedures are described below.

Differential Reinforcement of Alternative Behavior Plus Extinction

1) Short sessions of 5 to 10 minutes are conducted.
2) Before the session starts, the student is told that if he does not want to do the task, he can ask for a break or hand the teacher a break card.
3) The math work that is correlated with the unwanted behavior is presented.

4) The student is allowed to have a break from the work for 30 seconds when he asks or touches the break card.
5) The student is reminded every 30 seconds that if he needs a break, he can ask for one (antecedent strategy).
6) The work is re-presented after the 30 second break.
7) When the unwanted behavior occurs, he is physically guided to touch the break card or to ask for a break.
8) This cycle is repeated until the end of the session.
9) Several sessions are conducted until a pattern emerges.
10) As low rates of the unwanted behavior occur consistently, the sessions are lengthened.

Important Considerations

A consequence analysis is appropriate for behaviors that occur at relatively high rates prior to and during the assessment process. Behaviors must occur frequently enough for an efficient and productive assessment. It is important to note that an experimental consequence analysis, as described above, is not always a good option for students with brain injuries because their unwanted behavior oftentimes occurs at a low rate. And more importantly, the analysis relies on the occurrence of problem behavior which may be dangerous and hard to manage. Finally, in some cases, the student actually learns new and problematic patterns of behavior.

Experimental Sessions

Experimental analysis sessions can be conducted either in barren session rooms or in the naturalistic settings in which the behavior occurs. They can be brief, with only 8 sessions, or extended with 40-60 sessions. The materials required to do the analysis are the data collection materials (i.e., hand-held computer, paper and pencil, timer), a scripted session description, and condition materials related to the task itself (i.e., academic tasks, toys). If possible, experimental functional analyses should be conducted only after indirect and direct assessment methods have identified the variables that most likely maintain the behavior.

Treatment Effects Analysis

Evaluation of treatment effects is another method of verifying the hypothesis regarding the functional relationship between the unwanted behavior and replicating or repeating the application of the intervention to determine whether it changes the behavior.

The next graph depicts a treatment analysis with a reversal demonstrated for the example above.

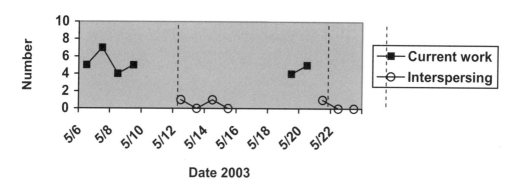

In many situations, a reversal is either not possible because of limited resources or because it would be unethical. For example, if the unwanted behavior results in injury either to the student or staff, it would be unethical to withdraw the successful treatment and allow the behavior to potentially resume and cause further injury.

Behavioral Assessment and the Individualized Education Plan (IEP)

Behavioral assessment can make significant contributions to the development of a student's Individualized Education Plan by identifying the student's behavioral excesses and deficits. It is essential that educators, parents, and other professionals understand the regulations and rights that students are afforded. The Individuals with Disabilities Education Act (IDEA or Public Law 101-476) is one such law that should be at the forefront for all those involved in educating students with disabilities.

IDEA supports behavioral assessment in two ways. First, if a student is suspended from school due to unwanted behavior, IDEA requires that a functional behavioral assessment be conducted. Second, the law states that functional behavioral assessment is a preferred method for developing the goals and objectives in an IEP. Parents, educators, and professionals should refer to special education policy and legislation to know their rights regarding behavioral assessment and education plans.

In some cases, a thorough behavioral assessment that is incorporated into the IEP may actually determine that the student's needs cannot be met in the current placement. If this is the case, the behavioral assessment may save the school district, family, and most importantly, the student valuable instructional time and money.

Using Behavioral Assessment to Structure the Classroom

In addition to providing valuable information for the development of the IEP, behavioral assessment can help the teacher arrange the classroom environment to best meet the student's needs. For instance, a behavioral assessment may suggest that the student would benefit from any of the following environmental arrangements:

- Instructional aide to assist with note taking
- Modified or increased ancillary therapies
- Desk placed away from doors, windows, and specific peers
- Difficult assignments presented in small parts
- Minimal distractions (i.e., noise)

The incorporation of a behavioral assessment in the IEP is an essential and important piece to an already challenging process for students who have experienced a brain injury. It is important for educators and families to know student rights under IDEA and to insist on a behavioral assessment when challenging behaviors emerge or when a student's educational opportunities have been significantly modified (i.e., due to suspension).

Behavioral Assessment

Diagram of Least to Most Valid Method

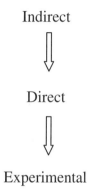

Indirect

Direct

Experimental

Diagram of Implementation

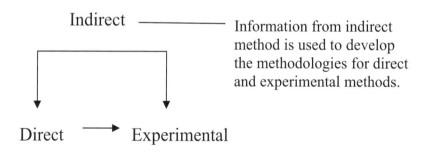

Information from indirect method is used to develop the methodologies for direct and experimental methods.

Behavioral Assessment

Method	Types	Information Gained	Validity	Resources Needed
Indirect	Questionnaires *Motivation Assessment Scale (MAS)* *Functional Analysis Screening Tool (FAST)* *Aberrant Behavior Checklist* Structured Interview	Potential environmental variables that maintain the target behavior. These variables include: When, where, with whom, and how often behavior occurs What happens before and after the behavior occurs From this information, a hypothesis about the function of the behavior can be developed. This information is used to determine when, where, and how to conduct direct assessment.	Low	Minimal
Direct / Descriptive	Antecedent Behavior Consequence (ABC) Analysis Scatter Plot Assessment	Data on specific variables that are thought to maintain the behavior are collected via direct observation of the target behavior. This information is used to design the conditions of the experimental analysis.	Moderate to High	Moderate
Experimental Analysis / Functional Analysis	Consequence Analysis Antecedent Analysis Treatment Effects Analysis	Tests the hypothesis generated by the indirect/direct methods regarding the effects of antecedents and/or consequences on the target behavior.	High	Extensive

Tests the hypothesis regarding the functional relationship between environmental variables and the behavior by examining the effects of the treatment on the behavior.

Validity Scale: High, Moderate, Low   Resource Scale: Extensive, Moderate, Minimal

Chapter 7
Practical Behavior Change Strategies: Manipulating Antecedents

Definition and Rationale

Antecedent-based interventions involve changing the events or variables that exist *before* the behavior occurs. These environmental changes *decrease* the likelihood of a challenging behavior occurring and *increase* the likelihood of a desired behavior occurring. Examples of antecedent-based interventions (also referred to as antecedent control) include the following:

- Providing reminders for upcoming tasks
- Reducing task demands
- Interspersing demands and social comments
- Choice-making

Recently, there has been an increasing emphasis on antecedent-based interventions in the fields of behavior analysis and brain injury rehabilitation. This focus has evolved from research that has demonstrated that antecedent-based strategies can effectively change a variety of behaviors across many settings. These interventions have been successful with students with autism, learning disabilities and brain injuries.

Antecedent manipulation is the preferred method of intervention for students with memory deficits. This method is effective because it does not require students to remember or understand the consequences of their behavior. Visual schedules or organizers are examples of antecedent-based interventions that may help a student with memory deficits attend activities on time and complete required tasks.

Other advantages of antecedent control procedures are that they are relatively easy to implement and can be done without confronting or punishing the student. Unlike consequence-based interventions, antecedent manipulation involves arranging the environment to promote positive interactions and skill development before the behavior occurs rather than after. This is done by making changes to such things as the seating arrangement, amount of work presented at one time, and the way in which a transition is communicated. Several practical antecedent-based strategies are described below.

> **Practical Antecedent-Based Strategies**
>
> ❑ Interspersing preferred and nonpreferred activities
> ❑ Reducing task requirements
> ❑ Imbedding demands within the context of social comments or conversations
> ❑ Using organizers and written reminders
> ❑ Self-monitoring

Interspersing Preferred and Nonpreferred Activities

Behavioral research has shown that students are more likely to engage in nonpreferred activities *if preferred activities precede and follow them.* Interspersing preferred and nonpreferred activities creates what is called ***behavioral momentum***. In everyday terms, behavioral momentum provides opportunities for the individual to "get into the swing of things". Students typically engage in nonpreferred tasks and activities when they are imbedded with highly motivating tasks and activities. This may be true because presentation of the preferred task reinforces or rewards the individual for completing the less preferred task.

❖ **Individuals with memory impairments may benefit from a visual schedule that shows the sequence of preferred and nonpreferred activities.**

Reducing Task Requirements

Sometimes unwanted behaviors occur immediately following an instruction or before a nonpreferred activity is about to begin. One method of decreasing those behaviors is to *shorten the amount of time that the student is required to be engaged in the task.* This technique may be helpful when problem behaviors occur during lengthy academic tasks or less preferred outings. Time on task is gradually increased or faded back to the original task requirement. For example, shortened outings in the grocery store may help family members avoid a difficult and embarrassing tantrum episode within the community. Over time, the duration of the outings may be systematically increased while maintaining a zero rate of problem behavior. This intervention has been used to decrease many behaviors (Kennedy, 1994).

Imbedding Social Comments

Another technique is to *reduce the number of demands and to present demands in the context of social comments*. Again, the demands are gradually faded back into the student's task requirements once the behaviors are effectively reduced. For instance, a student who has verbal outbursts when asked to do chores may be engaged in a conversation before being asked to do each chore. The student is then rewarded with another conversation after the chore is completed.

In one case, obscenity was successfully reduced with an adult with a brain injury (Pace, Ivancic, and Jefferson, 1994). After a functional behavior assessment found that obscene language functioned to escape demands or tasks, the number of demands/tasks was reduced. In addition, demands were presented in the context of continuous conversations. At first, the rate of social comments was greater than the rate of demands. Once the participant's obscenity decreased to zero, the ratio gradually reversed to the baseline rate of demand presentation. The number of obscenities remained at zero as the demands were increased.

Manipulating Task Difficulty

When challenging behaviors are exhibited during specific tasks, the task itself should be examined. It may be either too difficult or too easy. If the task is too difficult, it may be presented in smaller components (this is called a task analysis). Each component of the task is taught separately and easier and more difficult parts of the task are interspersed. In addition, task completion is rewarded with access to preferred activities and praise. The task may also be presented in a different format. Both the format and the task content may incorporate the student's interests. For instance, math problems can be presented one at a time in the context of a story. Or the topic of a writing assignment may refer to the student's favorite movie.

Using Organizers, Visual Schedules, and Written Reminders

Many people use some form of "To Do" lists, post-it notes, and organizers to keep track of appointments, birthdays, groceries, etc. It is difficult to remember everything that should be accomplished each day and each week. Imagine having a memory deficit. Remembering those important things can be near to impossible without some kind of visual support.

Written reminders have been used to modify work-related behaviors. One study found that posting a written reminder reduced the rate of unauthorized breaks with a 25-year old male (Zencius, Wesolowski, Burke, and McQuade, 1989). The written reminder to ask permission for taking breaks was placed above the workstation. With the reminder, the number and length of unauthorized breaks decreased to zero.

Self-monitoring

Academic behaviors are a primary focus of behavior support plans for students with brain injuries. Academic tasks are often difficult because of impairments in cognition, memory, attention, planning, organizing, and regulating behavior. Self-management techniques have been shown to improve academic behaviors with many populations. These techniques include self-monitoring, self-graphing and self-reinforcement.

For example, during a self-monitoring activity, students record whether or not they are on-task every 10 minutes during independent work time. At the end of the day, they graph their behavior. Alternatively, students record the number of assignments completed each day.

❖ **With self-monitoring, behavior often changes without any additional intervention as a result of students collecting their own data.**

Summary

Reducing task demands, presenting demands in the context of social comments, simplifying tasks, and incorporating preferred topics or interests are techniques that may reduce challenging behaviors associated with demand situations. In addition, visual schedules, reminders, and self-monitoring may increase on-task behavior and task completion. These are just a few of the many behavior change strategies that involve manipulating antecedents. Antecedent-based strategies can be implemented alone or in conjunction with other antecedent or consequence-based strategies.

Chapter 8
Practical Behavior Change Strategies:
Providing Positive Consequences

Reinforcement

Behavior analysts are well known for their use of interventions that involve manipulating the consequences, or events that follow behavior. Reinforcement procedures have been so successful in significantly improving behaviors that few behavioral interventions do not include some type of reinforcement procedure.

Providing reinforcers immediately following the target behavior is one way to increase the likelihood that the behavior will occur again. This is called *positive reinforcement*.

❖ **"Positive reinforcement is the most widely applied principle of behavior; it is one of the cornerstones upon which applied behavior analysts have built the technology of behavior change." (Cooper, Heron, & Heward, 1987, pp. 257)**

Taking a student away from an unpleasant event or location, removing an unwanted item, such as a task, or stopping a nonpreferred activity as a result of a behavior also functions to increase the behavior. This is called *negative reinforcement.*

❖ **As a result of negative reinforcement, a student is highly likely to exhibit the same behavior in the future simply because the behavior successfully ended the undesired situation.**

The Principle of Reinforcement

The principle of reinforcement describes (1) what happens in the environment following the occurrence of a behavior *and* (2) how the behavior changes as a result of that event. In order for reinforcement to occur, something is added or taken away from the environment with a resulting increase in the target behavior. The following chart summarizes positive and negative reinforcement.

Type of Reinforcement	Operation	Function
Positive Reinforcement	Something is added (+)	The behavior increases
Negative Reinforcement	Something is removed (-)	The behavior increases

As the table shows, when something is added or removed from the environment and a behavior increases, the behavior has been reinforced. If the behavior does not improve, reinforcement has not occurred.

Example of Positive Reinforcement

Consider children who do not do any chores. Many parents begin offering rewards to motivate their children to help out around the house. Some respond well to this reward and do their chores every week. Other children find chores so unpleasant that money is not enough. These children continue to avoid their chores even though they could earn a reward.

In the first case, reinforcement has occurred because the children started doing chores after the reward system was in place. In the latter case, reinforcement has not occurred because the behavior of doing chores has not increased as a result of the potential reward.

Example of Negative Reinforcement

Consider a child who tantrums on every trip to the grocery store. The parent removes the child from the grocery if the tantrum continues for so long that the parent becomes frustrated and walks out without any groceries. This is an example of negative reinforcement. In this case, the unpleasant situation (the grocery store) is removed following the occurrence of the behavior (tantrum). The child was successful. The tantrum resulted in leaving the grocery store. Therefore, the child is likely to tantrum again during the next visit to the grocery store.

Reinforcers

One of the most important tasks for educators, professionals, and parents is to determine how to motivate their students. Motivating students is essential to their success. This is challenging because many students are motivated by different things. Research shows that caregiver and staff opinions about what students find rewarding are often inconsistent with what students select as their reinforcers.

The most common reinforcers are preferred foods, activities, toys, attention and social interaction. It is important to remember, however, that not everything that is preferred actually increases behavior. An item acts as a reinforcer only if it increases the behavior it follows. *Preference assessments* are helpful to determine what items, events, or situations are most likely to function as reinforcers. With minimal time and effort, these assessments can greatly enhance the success of teaching programs as well as behavioral interventions designed to decrease unwanted behavior.

There are many different types of preference assessments. Some assessments involve presenting the student with a few to several choices. The items that are chosen the most are rated as ***most preferred***. The items that are chosen the least are rated as ***least preferred***.

The Two-Item Forced Choice Preference Assessment is one type of assessment. For this assessment, the student is asked to choose from two items. These items (i.e., food, toys, activities, etc.) are selected by asking staff and/or caregivers to identify what they think are preferred items. This can be done through interviews or by asking them to generate a list of preferred items. As mentioned above, selected items are considered to be most, moderate, or preferred based on a scale. For example, items that are selected over 80% or greater of opportunities are the most preferred and items that are selected less than 50% of opportunies are the least preferred. An example of the Two-Item Forced Choice Preference Assessment is provided in the appendix.

There are also preference assessments that involve observing what students do during their free time. For this type of assessment, an observer records the amount of time that the student engages in the activity.

When the most preferred items are presented following the occurrence of a behavior, the future occurrence of the behavior will most likely increase. Likewise, the least preferred items are probably not going to increase the behavior they follow. Therefore, the most preferred items are highly likely to function as reinforcers. In other words, there is a better chance of motivating students to behave appropriately or to accomplish tasks when highly preferred items are presented as rewards.

If preferences change weekly or even daily, it is necessary to conduct frequent preference assessments. Varying preferences are common among children and adolescents with brain injuries. They tend to get too much of a reinforcer so that it loses its effectiveness. This is called ***satiation***. As a result of "having too much," the reinforcer is no longer effective and the target behavior does not change. When this occurs, people often assume that the procedure failed. However, it may be that the reinforcer lost its efficacy.

❖ **The potency of the reinforcer can be maintained and satiation reduced by restricting access to the reinforcer to intervention times only and varying the reinforcer over the course of an intervention.**

Reinforcement Procedures

There are many ways to use reinforcement to increase behaviors. These procedures can be complex or simple and may involve one or more individuals. Careful assessment of the environmental variables that maintain the behavior should be done prior to designing the treatment. This ensures that the intervention:

1) matches the function of the behavior and
2) is consistent with the individual's cognitive abilities, preferences, social skills, and personal interests.

Positive Feedback Using Praise

Providing positive reinforcement through verbal positive feedback, or praise, is one of the most powerful ways to maintain or improve behavior. It can improve behaviors such as cooperation, attending, and positive social interactions.

❖ **Children and adolescents with brain injuries typically respond well to positive feedback that is immediate, sincere, age-appropriate, consistent, and behavior specific.**

It is most effective to follow these simple rules when providing praise:

1) provide praise and attention for the specific behavior targeted for improvement and
2) avoid praising or attending to behaviors that are intended to be reduced.

These rules will help you communicate to the student which behaviors will be rewarded and which behaviors will not be rewarded.

It is also important to remember that verbal positive reinforcement may *not* be reinforcing to everyone. For some students, praise may actually not be preferred. This is why it is important to conduct a preference assessment to determine whether or not praise functions as a reinforcer. For students who prefer to receive positive feedback, staff and family members can seize as many opportunities as possible to praise appropriate behaviors. This creates a positive environment for everyone present.

> **Positive Feedback should be . . .**
> Immediate
> Sincere
> Age-appropriate
> Consistent
> Behavior specific

Differential Reinforcement

This is a positive procedure that reduces behavior without causing the individual to lose anything or be punished. Differential reinforcement has been used in many settings including the classroom, home, workplace, and community. This intervention is highly preferred because "it maintains a positive environment" and is easy to implement (Cooper, et al., pp. 392).

There are several types of differential reinforcement procedures:
Differential reinforcement of other or zero rates of behavior
Differential reinforcement of incompatible or alternative behavior
Differential reinforcement of low rates of behavior

Differential Reinforcement of Other or Zero Behavior (DRO)

Definition   The reinforcer is provided after a specific period of time in which the target behavior is not observed. If the behavior occurs during the interval, the interval starts again. It is best to start with a short interval that produces a zero rate of behavior. The interval is then gradually increased until the behavior is either significantly reduced or eliminated.

Example John receives additional recess time only if he does not talk out during math class.

Differential Reinforcement of Lower Rates of Behavior (DRL)
Definition The reinforcer is provided after a period of time in which the occurrences of the target behavior do not exceed a specified criterion. The criterion is gradually decreased until the desired rate is achieved.

Example Alice receives 10 minutes of one-to-one time with staff only if she swears less than five times during during the lunch hour.

Differential Reinforcement of Incompatible Behavior (DRI) or Differential Reinforcement of Alternative Behavior (DRA)
Definition The reinforcer is provided for a behavior that is incompatible or alternative to the target behavior. The incompatible behavior is a behavior that cannot be done while exhibiting the target behavior. Alternative behavior is an appropriate behavior that replaces the inappropriate behavior but is not incompatible with the inappropriate behavior.

Example *Incompatible:* Tommy gets a sticker if he sits on his hands rather than tapping his fingers on the desk during the history lecture.
Alternative: Joan and Lori are given extra recess time if they cooperate instead of argue during a group project.

Shaping
Shaping is a highly preferred method for establishing a new behavior or modifying an existing behavior. The procedure starts with a response that is already in the person's repertoire. Responses that are closer and closer to the desired response are then reinforced. Many teachers, athletic coaches, and even parents use shaping daily to gradually improve students' behaviors.

For example, one of Tori's goals is to walk the entire length of a 5-foot balance beam. In the beginning, she can only balance briefly (about 1 second) on one leg. During the shaping process, her physical therapist requires her to stand on one leg for longer and longer periods of time before getting a break. Gradually, Tori learns to shift her balance from one leg to the other. She then learns to do this on the balance beam. Eventually, Tori is given a break only after she walks the entire length of the balance beam.

In another example, one of Joan's goals is to learn to write her name. In the beginning, she can only draw a line down the page. Thus, her teacher initially praises Joan just for drawing a vertical line. Gradually the teacher requires Joan to write more and more of her name before providing praise.

Prior to implementing a shaping procedure, the team must identify and define (1) the initial behavior to be reinforced and (2) the terminal or goal behavior. The initial response may be very similar to the final desired response or may not resemble the final desired response at all. It is important that the initial reinforced response already occurs without additional learning. Hence, shaping capitalizes on a student's strengths rather than on weaknesses.

Shaping may also be used to improve . . .

- Athletic performance
  (i.e., a baseball player's swing, or a figure skater's turn, a dancer's leap)
- Speech production
- Play skills
- Drawing and handwriting

Summary

Positive feedback is a simple procedure that can motivate students. Differential reinforcement is a variation of a simple reinforcement procedure. This procedure involves providing reinforcement according to specific rules. For example, differential reinforcement of low rates of behavior involves providing reinforcement after a period of time in which the number of occurrences of a particular behavior does not exceed a predetermined criteria. Shaping involves reinforcing successive approximations of the target behavior until the terminal behavior is observed. Shaping may be helpful for improving handwriting, gross motor skills and speech.

The rehabilitation or educational team may develop a behavioral treatment package that includes manipulation of both antecedents and consequences. Several procedures may be combined to simultaneously decrease problem behaviors and increase appropriate behaviors.

❖ **Just remember to follow the behavior plan *all the time* and in *all situations.* The success of any behavior change procedure depends on it!**

Chapter 9
Case Studies

Case Study: Antecedent-Based Treatment

John was a 14-year-old male who had a traumatic brain injury when he was six years old as the result of a motor vehicle crash. The records indicate that he had a closed head injury to the frontal lobe area. His teachers reported that he often became frustrated in class and left his seat to go into the hallway. While in the hallway, he disrupted other students. Due to these unwanted behaviors, John was suspended from school and was not allowed to return without a treatment plan. Subsequently, a behavior analyst was called to determine how to improve John's behavior so that he could return to school and be successful.

The behavior analyst began by conducting thorough indirect assessments that included structured interviews with teachers and questionnaires that asked teachers about when, where, and how often the behavior occurred. Results from these assessments suggested that the bolting occurred when John was presented with lengthy assignments, such as reading comprehension. However, the behavior analyst conducted an antecedent analysis to evaluate the effects of the length of academic tasks on bolting behavior. The following table and graph show the results of this analysis:

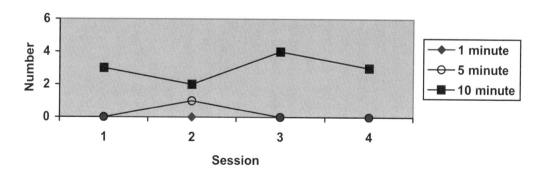

Condition: Length of task antecedent analysis

Student: John

Target behavior: Bolting

Operational definition: Any instance in which the student stands up from his seat and takes more than one step away from his seat without returning.

Data collection: The frequency of bolting is collected after 1, 5, and 10 minutes after he has begun working on the assignment.

Time Interval	Session 1	Session 2	Session 3	Session 4
1 minute into task	0	0	0	0
5 minutes into task	0	1	0	0
10 minutes into task	111	11	1111	111

    This assessment indicates that as tasks reached the 10-minute mark, bolting behavior occurred at significantly higher rates than when the task lasted one to five minutes. The treatment that was developed involved reducing the duration of the task so that minimal behaviors occurred during the assignment. The duration of the task was gradually increased until John could tolerate tasks up to 15 minutes without bolting.

    In addition, John received verbal praise every five minutes for remaining in his seat and working on his assigned tasks. This intervention is called *reducing task demands plus differential reinforcement*. By analyzing and then modifying antecedent variables, John's bolting behavior decreased while his performance on lengthy assignments improved. Because John no longer exhibited disruptive behavior, he was successfully transitioned back to school and was eventually able to tolerate tasks that lasted up to 45 minutes.

Case Study: Consequence-Based Treatment

Fred is a 16-year-old boy with significant brain damage due to anoxia from a near drowning incident when he was 14 years old. His unwanted behavior was aggression. This had become so severe that he was moved from the group home program to a psychiatric hospital. Indirect assessment measures indicated that the aggressive behavior might be functioning to enable him to escape demands. However, direct assessment measures indicated that the unwanted behavior occurred during periods of low staff attention.

Although the behavior occurred only occasionally, the aggression was intense. Therefore, an antecedent choice assessment was conducted. During this assessment, Fred was given a choice of situations. On one side of the room, he could spend time with a staff member, but that staff member would ask him to complete relatively easy academic or vocational tasks. On the other side of the room, he could be alone with some of his preferred games. Fred consistently chose the side of the room with the staff present, even though he was required to complete tasks. This information was consistent with results from the direct assessments.

A treatment effects analysis was then performed. In this analysis, the effects of a *differential reinforcement of (DRO) zero rates of behavior* treatment procedure on the target behavior (aggression) were evaluated. During this program, John received ten minutes of individual staff attention if he did not engage in aggressive behavior for one hour. He also received verbal praise every fifteen minutes for following his activity schedule. The criteria for receiving ten minutes of staff attention was gradually increased from one to two hours and then to three hours as he successfully refrained from unwanted behaviors. Fred eventually transitioned back to a group home in the community and later returned to his family's home.

Conclusion

Many children and adolescents with brain injuries experience cognitive, physical, sensory, psychosocial, and behavioral changes that affect every facet of life. They often exhibit unwanted behaviors (i.e., aggression, inattention, bolting, and inappropriate language) that can negatively impact everyday functioning. These behaviors limit their participation in rehabilitation, home, school, and community activities. Applied Behavior Analysis (ABA) offers a scientific methodology for examining, measuring, and treating behavioral deficits. This methodology includes operational definitions of goals and treatments, functional outcomes, and systematic assessments.

A primary focus of behavior analysis (and brain injury rehabilitation) is the reduction of aberrant behaviors and the acquisition of functional skills. According to ABA, functional behavior assessment is central to accomplishing these goals. Behavioral assessment can be easily incorporated into the standard series of neuropsychological, sensory, and motor assessments that are used to develop rehabilitation and educational treatment plans. This assessment methodology involves a systematic analysis of the environmental conditions that lead to the occurrence of the unwanted behavior. The purpose of this assessment is to design treatment procedures that address those environmental variables. By doing so, treatment is more likely to be both effective and efficient.

There are many effective behavior change procedures that can be applied to help students with brain injuries improve academic performance, increase participation in community activities, experience positive social interactions, and eliminate maladaptive habits. When determining behavior change procedures, the rehabilitation or educational team must consider many factors, including available resources, likely positive effects, possible unwanted effects, skills of behavior change agents (i.e., family and staff), support in evidence-based research, and ethical issues.

Both antecedent-based interventions (such as demand fading and visual organizers) and consequence-based interventions (such as differential reinforcement and praise) have been shown to be effective with individuals with brain injuries. These interventions require staff and/or family members to plan ahead. They may need to adapt academic tasks, make adjustments to the daily schedule, or create materials. This may seem like a lot of work. However, by doing the preparations up front, many severe challenging behavioral episodes can be avoided. Thus, children and adolescents with brain injuries may be more able to achieve rehabilitation goals, be successful in school, participate in community activities, and cultivate positive and fulfilling relationships with friends and family.

Glossary of Terms

Antecedent
The events that exist before a behavior occurs.

Antecedent analysis
This type of assessment involves systematically presenting specific antecedent variables (i.e., amount of academic work, the duration of the task, and the number of students at a table) that have been identified to be associated with the unwanted behavior.

Behavioral assessment
A systematic method of examining the variables that affect the occurrence and nonoccurrence of behavior. Indirect, direct, and experimental analyses are types of behavioral assessment.

Behavioral momentum
The tendency of individuals to engage in nonpreferred tasks if preferred tasks precede and follow nonpreferred tasks. The individual "gets into the swing of things."

Consequence
The events that follow the behavior.

Consequence analysis
A consequence analysis is a type of assessment that involves systematically presenting specific consequence variables that have been identified to be associated with the unwanted behavior.

Differential reinforcement
Positive procedure that involves reinforcing only wanted behaviors not attending to unwanted behaviors.

Differential reinforcement of incompatible behavior
The reinforcer is provided for a behavior that is incompatible to the target behavior.

Differential reinforcement of low rates of behavior
The reinforcers are provided after a period of time in which the occurrences of the target behavior do not exceed a specified criterion.

Differential reinforcement of other behavior
The reinforcer is provided after a specific period of time in which the target behavior is not observed.

Direct assessment
Also called descriptive methods, these are techniques that use direct observation of the unwanted behavior in the environmental setting in which it naturally occurs. Examples include an ABC or Scatter plot analysis.

Duration
The time between the onset of a behavior and offset of behavior. Duration is a response measure that is used to measure continuous or episodic behaviors.

Extinction
Withholding reinforcement for a previously reinforced behavior to reduce the occurrence of the behavior.

Frequency
The number of times a behavior occurs in a period of time. Frequency is a response measure that is used to measure behavior that has a definite beginning and end and occurs at a moderate rate.

Functional analysis/assessment
Describes techniques or methods that identify behavioral function. In other words, what purpose does the unwanted behavior serve and under what conditions does it occur? Also called behavioral assessment or functional behavioral assessment.

Indirect assessment
These are techniques that rely on non-direct means of gathering behavioral information in order to form a hypothesis about the function of the unwanted behavior. Examples include interviews, rating scales, and records review.

Individualized Education Plan (IEP)
This plan is a legal document and is developed for each child who is found eligible for special education and/or related services under the state's Law of Education. This plan includes the child's current abilities, short-term and long-term objectives, services to be provided, and methods for evaluation.

Interval recording
A recording method in which the observer records whether or not the behavior occurred during a specific time period.

Momentary time sampling
A recording method that measures the target behaviors that are observed at the end of an interval. It is an excellent method to use when recording classroom behaviors.

Operational definition
Definition of the target behavior that is objective, unambiguous, measurable, and observable. It includes examples of what the behavior is and what it is not.

Partial interval recording
A type of interval recording method in which the behavior is recorded if it occurs at all during the interval.

Preference assessment
Preference assessments are techniques the enable the assessor to identify potential reinforcers or what the child prefers.

Reinforcement
An intervention that involves manipulating the consequences, or events that follow target behaviors. It may be positive or negative.

Reversal design
Demonstrates the effect of an intervention by implementing an intervention then removing the intervention, and then replicating or repeating the application of the intervention to determine whether it occasions a change in the behavior (also called an ABAB Design).

Scatter plot
Recording the time of day the unwanted behavior occurs across successive days. These patterns of unwanted behavior are correlated with time of day or events in the environment.

Shaping
A behavioral technique that is used to develop or improve behaviors. It involves reinforcing successive approximations of the target behavior until the terminal behavior is exhibited.

Topography
The form of a behavior or what the behavior "looks like."

Treatment effects analysis
The hypothesized function is examined by implementing a treatment and then evaluating its effects on the unwanted behavior.

Whole interval recording
A type of interval recording method that measures continuous or highly repetitive behaviors, such as self-stimulatory behavior. In this method, the occurrence of behavior is recorded only if it is observed throughout the entire interval.

References

Aman, M.G.,& Singh, N.N. (1994). The Aberrant Behavior Checklist: Community. East Aurora, NY: Slosson.

Axelrod, S. & Rolider, A. (2000). How to teach self-control through trigger analysis. How to manage behavior series. Austin, Texas: PRO-ED, Inc.

Braumling-McMorrow, D., Niemann, G.W., & Savage, R. (Eds.) (1998). Training Manual for Certified Brain Injury Specialists (CBIS), (Available from the American Academy for the Certification of Brain Injury Specialists, Alexandria, Virginia).

Brotherton, F.A., Thomas, L.L., Wisotzek, I.E., & Milan, M.A. (1988). Social skills training in the rehabilitation of patients with traumatic closed head injury. Archives of Physical Medicine and Rehabilitation, 69, 827-832.

Bruce, S. & Selznick, L. (2003). The role of functional behavior assessment in children's brain injury rehabilitation. Brain Injury Source 6(3), 32-37.

Cooper, Heron, & Heward (1987). Applied behavior analysis. New Jersey: Prentice Hall. Deaton, A.V. (1994). Changing behaviors of students with acquired brain injuries. In R. C. Savage & G. F. Wolcott (Eds.), Educational dimensions of acquired brain injury, 257-274. Austin, Texas: PRO-ED, Inc.

Department of Health and Human Services (1989). Interagency Head Injury Task Force Report. Washington, D.C.; Department of Health and Human Services.

DePompei, R and Blosser, J. (2000). Communication – how communication changes over time. Wake Forest, NC: Lash and Associates Publishing.

Feeney, TJ and Urbanczyk, B (1994). "Behavior as Communication" in eds. R.Savage and G.Wolcott . Educational dimensions of acquired brain injury. Austin, TX: PRO-ED.

Feeney, T.F. & Ylvisaker, M. (1995). Choice and routine: antecedent behavioral interventions for adolescents with severe traumatic brain injury. Journal of Head Trauma Rehabilitation, 10(3), 67-86.

Fisher, W., Piazza, C.C., Bowman, L.G., Hagopian, L.P., Owns, J.C., & Slevin, I. (1992). A comparison of two approaches for assessing reinforcers for persons with severe and profound disabilities. Journal of Applied Behavior Analysis, 25, 491-498.

Gajar, A., Schloss, P.J., Schloss, C.N., & Thompson, C.K. (1984). Effects of feedback and self-monitoring on head trauma youths' conversation skills. Journal of Applied Behavior Analysis, 17, 353-358.

Green, C.W., Reid, D. H., White, L.K., Halford, R.C., Brittain, D.P., & Gardner, S.M. (1988). Identifying reinforcers for persons with profound handicaps: Staff opinion versus systematic assessment of preferences. Journal of Applied Behavior Analysis, 21, 31-43.

Hart, T., & Jacobs, H. (1993). Rehabilitation and management of behavioral disturbances following frontal lobe injury. Journal of Head Trauma Rehabilitation, 8, 1-12.

Iwata, B.A., Dorsey, M.F., Slifer, K.J., Bauman, K.E., & Richman, G.S. (1994). Toward a functional analysis of self-injury. Journal of Applied Behavior Analysis, 27, 197-209.

Jacobs, H. E. (1988). Yes, behavior analysis can help, but do you know how to harness it? Brain Injury, 2(4), 339-346.

Jacobs, H.E. (1993). Behavior analysis and brain injury rehabilitation: people, principles, and programs. Gaithersburg, Maryland: Aspen Publishers, Inc.

Kazdin, A.E. (1982). Single-case research designs: Methods for clinical and applied settings. New York: Oxford University Press.

Kennedy, C.H. (1994). Manipulating antecedent conditions to alter the stimulus control of problem behavior. Journal of Applied Behavior Analysis, 27, 161-170.

Lewis, F.D., Nelson, J., Nelson, J., & Reusink, P. (1988). Effects of three feedback contingencies on the socially inappropriate talk of a brain-injured adult. Behavior Therapy, 19, 203-211.

Luiselli, J.K. & Cameron, M.J. (1998). Antecedent control: innovative approaches to behavioral support. Baltimore, MD: Paul H. Brooks Publishing Co.

Martin, G. & Pear, J. (1999). Behavior modification: what it is and how to do it. New Jersey: Prentice Hall.

O'Reilly, M.F., Green, G., & Braunling-McMorrow, D. (1990). Self-administered written prompts to teach home accident prevention skills to adults with brain injury. Journal of Applied Behavior Analysis, 23(4), 431-446.

Pace, G.M. & Colbert, B. (1996). Role of behavior analysis in home and community-based neurological rehabilitation. Journal of Head Trauma Rehabilitation, 11 (1), 18-26.

Pace, G.M., Ivancic, M.T., Edwards, G.L., Iwata, B.A., & Page, T.J. (1985). Assessment of stimulus preference and reinforcer value with profoundly retarded individuals. Journal of Applied Behavior Analysis, 18, 249-255.

Pace, G.M., Ivancic, M.T., Jefferson, G. (1994). Stimulus fading as treatment for obscenity in a brain-injured adult. Journal of Applied Behavior Analysis, 27, 301-305.

Pace, G. M., & Nau, P.A. (1993). Behavior analysis in brain injury rehabilitation: Training staff to develop, implement, and evaluate behavior change programs. In Staff development and clinical intervention in brain injury rehabilitation (pp. 105-127). Gaithersburg, Maryland: Aspen Publishers, Inc.

Selznick, L. & Savage, R.C. (2000). Using self-monitoring procedures to increase on-task behavior with three adolescents with brain injury. Behavioral Interventions, 15, 1-17.

Silver, B.V., Boake, C., Cavazos, D.I. (1994). Improving functional skills using behavioral procedures in a child with anoxic brain injury. <u>Archives of Physical Medicine and Rehabilitation, 75,</u> 742-745.

Slifer, K.J., Cataldo, M.D., Battitt, R.L., Kane, A.C., Harrison, K.A., & Cataldo, M.F, (1993). Behavior analysis and intervention during hospitalization for brain trauma rehabilitation. <u>Archives of Physical Medicine and Rehabilitation, 74,</u> 810-817.

Slifer, K.J. & Kurtz, P.F. (1995). Behavioural training during acute brain trauma rehabilitatin: an empirical case study. <u>Brain Injury, 9,</u> 585-593.

Suzman, K.B., Morris, R.D., Morris, M.K., & Milan, M.A. (1997). Cognitive-behavioral remediation of problem solving deficits in children with acquired brain injury. <u>Journal of Behavioral Experimental Psychiatry, 28 (3),</u> 203-212.

Touchette, P.E., MacDonald, R.F., & Langer, S.N. (1985). A scatter plot for identifying stimulus control of problem behavior. *Journal of Applied Behavior Analysis, 18, 343-351.*

Wehman, P., West, M., Fry, R., Sherron, P., Groah, C., Kreutzer, J., & Sale, P. (1989). Effect of supported employment on the vocational outcomes of persons with traumatic brain injury. <u>Journal of Applied Behavior Analysis, 22(4),</u> 395-405.

Zencius, A.H., Wesolowski, M.D., Burke, W.H., McQuade, P., (1989). Antecedent control in the treatment of brain-injured clients. <u>Brain Injury, 3(2),</u> 199-205.

Resources for Information

Top 5 Websites on Behavior

Website	Description
www.abainternational.org	The Association for Applied Behavior Analysis website. This website provides basic information about ABA, membership, conferences and degree programs.
www.envmed.rochester.edu/wwwrap/behavior/jaba/jabahome.htm	Journal of Applied Behavior Analysis This website contains abstracts of journal articles that examine the effects behavioral procedures with a range of populations and behaviors.
www.bacb.com	This is the official website of Behavior Analyst Certificaiton Board,Inc.. It contains information regarding the certification process and the qualifications that certificants are required to meet and maintain. This site also maintains a list of Certified Behavior Analysts.
www.behavior.org	Cambridge Center for Behavioral Studies website. This website contains information, newsletters and publications related to the varying aspects of behavior analysis. Topics include: aging, safety, education, and parenting.

Top 5 Websites with Information on Brain Injury

Website	Description
www.biausa.org	Brain Injury Association of America's website has clinical information, research updates, policy bulletins, state resources and many useful links.
www.lapublishing.com	Lash and Associates Publishing/Training, Inc. has extensive information on the effects of brain injury on children and youth with a special product line on educating students with brain injury.
www.nichcy.org	The National Information Center on Children and Youth with Disabilities specializes in information for parents on their rights and responsibilities under the Individuals with Disabilities Education Act. There is a Fact Sheet on Traumatic Brain Injury and Resources by state.
www.cdc.gov/ncipc/factsheets/tbi.htm	Centers for Disease Control and Prevention - Traumatic Brain Injury presents research findings and prevention strategies, as well as publications on concussion and moderate to severe brain injury.
www.braininjuryresearch.org/tbi/b_queryItem.asp#search	National Database of Educational Resources on Traumatic Brain Injury has an extensive listing of publications compiled by the Rehabilitation Research and Training Center on Rehabilitation Interventions Following TBI and the Traumatic Brain Injury Technical Assistance Center.

Top 5 Books/Journal Articles

Book or Journal Article	Description
Axelrod, S. & Rolider, A. (2000). How to teach self-control through trigger analysis. <u>How to Manage Behavior Series</u>. Austin, Texas: PRO-ED, Inc.	Written for the classroom setting, this book discusses how to change problem behavior by assessing and changing antecedent variables or triggers.
Deaton, A.V. (1994). Changing behaviors of students with acquired brain injuries. In R. C. Savage & G. F. Wolcott (Eds.), <u>Educational Dimensions of Acquired Brain Injury</u> (pp. 257-274). Austin, Texas: PRO-ED, Inc.	This article discusses how to identify effective behavior change strategies and describes several strategies. It is well written and easy to understand.
Jacobs, H.E. (1993). <u>Behavior Analysis and Brain Injury Rehabilitation: People, Principles, and Programs</u>. Gaithersburg, Maryland: Aspen Publishers, Inc.	This manual offers a comprehensive explanation of behavior analysis, data collection, and behavior change procedures and includes several useful data sheets.
Pace, G.M. & Colbert, B. (1996). Role of behavior analysis in home and community-based neurological rehabilitation. <u>Journal of Head Trauma Rehabilitation</u>, 11 (1), 18-26.	This article presents a model of home and community-based rehabilitation that is based on the concepts and methodologies of behavior analysis. It illustrates how the behavioral approach can be used to design successful rehabilitation programs.
Zirpoli, T.J. & Melloy, K.J. (2001). <u>Behavior Management: Applications for Teachers.</u> Upper Saddle River, NJ: Prentice-Hall, Inc.	This book is intended for parents and professionals. It provides detailed explanations of the fundamentals of the behavioral approach, including behavioral assessment, and offers practical suggestions for how to improve behavior in classroom settings.

Appendix A: Blank Forms

List of blank forms included on the separate companion CD with PDF files formatted and reproducible on 8 ½ x 11 paper. These forms are not copyrighted and permission to make copies is granted by the publisher.

Scatter Plot Form..115
Antecedent Behavior Consequence (ABC) Form..117
Functional Assessment of Behavior Interview Form..118
Functional Assessment Interview Summary Form..131
Prioritizing Challenging Behaviors Worksheet...135
Challenging Behaviors Checklist...137
Prioritizing Adaptive Behaviors Worksheet..145
Two Item Stimulus Choice Preference: Assessment Instructions........................147
Preference Assessment Data Sheet..148
Preference Assessment 150

Appendix B
Sample Case Using Completed Forms

List of completed forms included on the separate companion CD with PDF files formatted and reproducible on 8 ½ x 11 paper.

John was hospitalized in November of his seventh grade year after sustaining a head injury to his frontal lobe when his all-terrain four-wheeler flipped over in a rock quarry where he was riding. He was not wearing a helmet. He spent 14 weeks in the hospital and then received tutoring in his home for the rest of the school year.

In September, eight months post-injury, John re-entered his former school to repeat the seventh grade. His teachers immediately noticed that he was much more distractible and irritable than prior to his injury when he was an average student, who was disruptive in class on occasion.

After the first week of school, John began bolting out of class when given academic tasks to complete. Due to this unwanted behavior, John was referred to the school psychologist, Mary Smith, who with the assistance of John's teachers and Mother, completed the following forms in this order:

Prioritizing Challenging Behaviors Worksheet..153
Challenging Behavior Checklist..154
Functional Assessment of Behavior Interview Form...161
Functional Assessment Interview Summary Form..173
ABC Assessment Form...175
Scatter Plot Assessment Form..177
Preference Assessment Data Sheet..179
Preference Assessment Summary..181